REMEMBER ETERNITY

J.E. STARKS-BROWN

authorHOUSE®

AuthorHouse™
1663 Liberty Drive
Bloomington, IN 47403
www.authorhouse.com
Phone: 1 (800) 839-8640

Published by AuthorHouse 01/18/2017

ISBN: 978-1-5246-6033-8 (sc)
ISBN: 978-1-5246-6032-1 (e)

Print information available on the last page.

Any people depicted in stock imagery provided by Thinkstock are models,
and such images are being used for illustrative purposes only.
Certain stock imagery © Thinkstock.

This book is printed on acid-free paper.

Because of the dynamic nature of the Internet, any web addresses or links contained in
this book may have changed since publication and may no longer be valid. The views
expressed in this work are solely those of the author and do not necessarily reflect the
views of the publisher, and the publisher hereby disclaims any responsibility for them.

Scripture quotations marked KJV are from the Holy Bible, King James Version
(Authorized Version). First published in 1611. Quoted from the KJV Classic
Reference Bible, Copyright © 1983 by The Zondervan Corporation.

Acknowledgement

To my brother Norman who faithfully took the time to read and encouraged me to continue in that which was given to me by the Author and Finisher of our faith. For this, I simply say Thank-you.

INTRODUCTION

"Remember Eternity", as its title suggests, is a reminder to us all that there is a life beyond this present one in which we now live. It is a fictional look into the lives of a group of not so ordinary Spirit filled people in the process of making preparations for eternity. Set in the city of Des Moines, Iowa in present day, the intention of "Remember Eternity is to cause the reader to get beyond what we see with our natural or carnal minds and to become focused on the spiritual and on that which is eternal.

The story line revolves around the day to day challenges in the family of Frances Michaels, her son Paul and three daughters, Irene, Christine, and Donna; their spouses Jane, Douglas James and Randy, respectively. As the mother of four and grandmother of forty-one, Frances is looked upon as a matriarchal symbol of God given wisdom coupled with rich experiences. She is ever nurturing, advising and whether solicited or no, her words are lovingly and at times reluctantly accepted.

Paul, the stern and serious high school principal, Douglas the prosperous insurance executive and minister, James the successful architect and Randy the transit coach operator, all come together to create a scenario of events and situations. As Paul, Christine and their spouses face the challenges of their interracial marriages they ultimately become stronger in their faith in God. He becomes their battle axe and strength in adversity when other extended family members come into play. Sensitive issues arise but are successfully overcome on a spiritual level, which is the basic foundation and theme of "Remember Eternity." It is intended to utilize and introduce a spiritual perspective in an increasingly Anti-Christ society and although unpopular and often tedious, doing it God's way insures victory.

"Men and brethren, what shall we do?"

Then Peter said unto them, Repent and be baptized every one of you in the name of Jesus Christ for the remission of sins and ye shall receive the Holy Ghost. (Acts 2:38 KJV).

For the Lord himself shall descend from heaven with a shout, with the voice of the archangel, and with the trump of God: and the dead in Christ shall rise first:

Then we which are alive and remain shall be caught up together with them in the clouds, to meet the Lord in the air: and so shall we ever be with the Lord. 1 Thessalonians 4,v 16, 17 (KJV)...

FOREWORD

In these perilous and uncertain times, there remains one undeniable fact that we all must face and that is Eternity. As we live our everyday lives, year in and year out, we are ever moving closer to the era where time will be an extinct entity. In our human natures, we tend to view Eternity as a fact that is eons away or something to be dealt with after we tend to our own temporal agendas.

The Word of God leaves no doubt about the two eternal destinations that we have the options to choose from. Eternal reward in Heaven or eternal damnation in Hell leaves no choice to the reasonable mind and this being said, it only makes sense to "Remember Eternity".

In this society, we are bombarded with countless winds of doctrine that have forms of godliness while denying the power thereof which is a danger to the eternal soul. Ephesians 4:5 (KJV) plainly states that there is One Lord, one faith, one baptism. This one Lord, Jesus Christ, commanded us in St. Matthew 28:19 to be baptized in the name of the Father (Jesus), the name of the Son (Jesus) and the name of the Holy Ghost (Jesus), not His titles. This was confirmed through the Apostle Peter on the Day of Pentecost (Acts 2:38), when three thousand souls were added on the Birth Day of the Church. The ingredients of genuine godly sorrow or repentance from sin, water baptism in the name of Jesus for the remission or removal of sin, coupled with the baptism of the Holy Ghost. The undeniable evidence of this second birth experience is the speaking in other tongues as the Spirit of God gives the utterance. There is no substitute for this awesome encounter with God that empowers the born again believer to overcome the sinful Adamic nature that we are all enter into this world with. It is not to be scoffed at or minimized by those who would downplay its significance or importance.

"Remember Eternity" opens with eighteen year old Janice Scott who impulsively leaves her home in Washington D.C. to join her cousins in Des Moines Iowa. While harboring a secret, she develops new relationships and begins to encounter situations that ultimately transform her from an angry and cynical teen-ager into a new creature in God. As one life touches another, circumstances evolve into a myriad of events that in time give God the glory for His wonderful works to the children of men.

Janice discovers the power of Agape' love through those that are Spirit filled while enduring several life changing hardships that forever change her perspective on life. Through these adversities, she begins to experience a father-daughter relationship that she was deprived of during her unstable childhood and this in turn enriches her spirit in a way that had been before unimaginable. Because of the God given wisdom and compassion of her surrogate father Douglas, she learns how to depend on the God of her salvation as she simultaneously begins to give of herself to others.

"Remember Eternity" is an intimate look into a family's struggles, victories, trials and tribulations of the righteous which are all a part of the sanctified set apart life that God is calling for in these troubling and stressful times.

CHAPTER 1

FEBRUARY 8, SUNDAY

"Is this James?"

"You got it, who is this?"

"This is Janice Scott, another cousin from D.C. and I need for you to come pick me up at the airport."

"Janice Scott?"

"Yeah, didn't 'Nita tell you that I was comin'?

"I don't know anything about this."

"She must not have believed me when I told her that I was runnin' away from home." "She dared me to do this but she should know better by now."

"C'mon James, we have to go and get her!" 'Nita yelled down the steps after overhearing the conversation.

"Hold up 'Nita, I can't do anything 'til I run this by Chris first."

"Run what by me, what's goin' on?" Chris asked from the kitchen.

"Janice just got here from Washington and she's at the airport." 'Nita began. "I dared her to do it but she's here and she needs for us to come and get her." She explained, trying to keep a straight face.

"How long is she plannin' to stay?"

"Until she leaves." "You don't understand, this is not a visit, this is a move." 'Nita told him. "And you can't let me stay in that big bedroom by myself so you might as well give in and let it happen."

"I'm leavin' this up to you honey, it doesn't really matter to me." James told her after a moment.

"Just go and get her and we'll talk about it when you get back." Chris reluctantly conceded. "But she needs to know that she might be doin' some babysittin' around here 'til she finds a job."

"I knew you'd see it my way and don't be such a worrywart, this'll be a good thing." 'Nita said as she got her coat from the front closet. "This house is big enough for one more so we'll just be one big happy family."

"'Nita how do you do this kind of stuff, this takes a lot of guts." James remarked half an hour later as they walked from the parking lot to the terminal.

"Don't you know by now that if your name is Scott, things like this come naturally?" "If you need to get somethin' done, you just do it without thinkin' about it too much because if you do, you'll lose your nerve." "Right?" "Right."

"What's your uncle gonna say?"

"He can't say too much, she's old enough to do what she wants." She came back. "Her eighteenth birthday was last week so she's just exercisin' her rights."

"So her and Sheila are a year apart."

"Exactly and I talked to her last Sunday and she said she was grown now and she wanted to prove it." "So I dared her to run away from home and fly here without tellin' anybody what she was doin' but I didn't think she would really do it." She added, starting to laugh. "I love it."

"What took you so long, I was about to call again to find out what happened." Janice said five minutes later as she approached them. "Hey you really are a white boy ain't you?" She asked James.

"He used to be."

"How come Chris didn't come, was she mad?"

"She wasn't mad but she said she would have more help around the house."

"How many kids do you have and how old are they?" Janice asked cautiously. "The last I heard Chris had a set of twins but that was four or five years ago."

"That was three babies ago, it's a total of seven of 'em but they know how to behave so don't have a stroke." 'Nita said. "They're in Sunday school every week so don't start trippin.'"

"Yeah that's another thing, I heard that everybody here goes to church eight days a week." "What's up with that?"

"Who told you that?" James asked her.

"I just heard some stuff through the grapevine so I'm not givin' away my sources but let me make this one thing clear." She said pausing. "I'll babysit your kids but ain't nobody gonna get me in church like that." She added defensively.

"Chill out Janice, it's not that deep." 'Nita told her as they approached the van. "But if you have a problem with stuff like that you need to stay away from Douglas cause he'll tell you like it is and keep on truckin.'"

"Wait a minute, who is Douglas?" Janice asked with disgust.

"Irene's husband so you have to run into him eventually."

"So what makes him think that he can be preachin' to folks that he doesn't even know?" She asked, raising her voice. "I know already that I can't deal with him, we gonna have some problems." She added. "And when I do see him, I'll just tell him from the start to stay out of my kool-aid."

"He won't bring it up unless you do." James told her as he put her luggage in the back.

"What-ever." She said. "Anyway am I gonna be sleepin' in the same room with a bunch of babies?" "Tell me now so I'll know what to expect". She said, purposely changing the subject.

"Nope this is the house that James and his sisters grew up in so it was built a thousand years ago when the bedrooms were the size of the Grand Canyon." 'Nita told her.

"What happened, did you inherit it or somethin'?"

"My mother put it up for sale when my father died and I bought it."

"Just had to keep it in the family huh?"

"Somethin' like that."

"So what kind of job can I find around here really quick?"

"You probably need to talk to Ruth or Sheila, both of them have good jobs and they can probably hook you up really quick." 'Nita answered her.

"I'll do anything except flip burgers, I'm better than that." "And I need to talk to 'em tonight, asap."

"They live with Aunt Frances and they're probably at church." "I'll text Ruth and let them know that you're here."

"Don't you think they're wonderin' where you are Janice?" Chris asked her an hour later at the kitchen table.

"I'm about to take care of that Chris, don't hyperventilate." She answered irritably. She said, getting her phone from her purse. "And maybe I should let 'em sweat for a minute." She added, laughing a little.

"Don't you think they're worried about you honey?" "They're gonna start to think somethin' happened to you and that's not a good feelin'."

"Somethin' did happen to me; I turned eighteen and it shouldn't matter to them what I do or don't do anymore." "But since you're lettin' me stay on such short notice, "I'll call 'em so you won't be trippin.'" "Where's your phone, mine just died."

"There's one upstairs if you want some privacy." James said, trying not to laugh.

"I hope they're not there so I can just leave 'em a voicemail." "I'm makin' it, don't worry about me, end of story".

CHAPTER 2

TUESDAY, FEBRUARY 10

"You know that I'm gonna have to dip into your business don't you?" Janice asked Tuesday night at the dinner table with Douglas and Irene.

"Why is that?"

"I just need to know how you can have a place like this with a stay at home wife and six kids". "People just don't do that anymore so you must be doin' somethin' illegal."

"If you have your priorities in the right place then the rest of it takes care of itself."

"It has to be more than that; what do you do, insurance?" Janice persisted.

"Somebody's been talkin' to you, I can tell."

"And you know it because if I'm gonna be livin' here for awhile I need to know who I'm dealin' with." She answered. "And so far, I think I know enough about Chris and James to get by so now it's your turn."

"She told me how you left home without tellin' anybody that you were leavin." Irene remarked.

"It's called doin' what you have to do and they know where I am now so that's all I'm sayin' about that." She said after a moment. "But I do need you to hook me up with a job and you look like the type that has connections." She told Douglas.

"What kind of work experience do you have?"

"I just graduated from high school so I can't have too much, you know what I'm sayin' Mr. Douglas?" She asked him. "And you look like somebody that has letters behind your name, am I right?"

"What does that look like?"

"Don't be playin' dumb, you know you got it goin' on." She told him. "And if you don't wanna talk about it, I can get it out of Irene over here." She said nudging her. "We're cousins, we can talk like that."

"Go to this website and fill out an application and we'll go from there." He said, writing on a napkin.

"Can I use you as a reference?" She persisted.

He didn't say anything but handed her a business card from his wallet.

"I knew it, Douglas Johnson C.L.U." She read out loud. "How did you find this dude?" She asked Irene.

"You really wanna know?"

Yeah I do because I heard from somebody that you're one of these people that has this saved from the streets story and I just wanna know how all this happened." She said, looking around.

"What else have you heard?" Douglas asked her. "Was it good, bad or indifferent?"

"I heard that you know how to shoot people down with the Bible if they don't agree with you." "What's up with that?" She fired back.

"I don't shoot people down but I will tell you the truth and if it offends you I don't have any control over that."

"So you're sayin' that you have a way of upsettin' people when it comes to religion?"

"I don't discuss religion because that's not what I'm about." He answered her. "My thing is if I have the chance to tell somebody about how the Lord got me off the streets, I have to tell it like it was and it wasn't religion that did it ma'am."

"What do you call it then?" She asked him as she began to become irritated with his responses.

"There's a difference in religion and salvation and that's what I have by doin' it the way God said do it." "He promised us the gift of the Holy Ghost and that's the power and strength He gave me to leave all of that stuff out there."

"So you just woke up one day and decided to go the meetin' one night cause your heart wasn't right?" Janice asked him with sarcasm in her voice.

"Do you really want the details?" He asked after a moment.

"Can't wait."

"I was on my way to a crack house with this motorcycle gang and I was high as a kite on a windy day." He began.

"You lyin', you are too smooth for that."

"And was goin' back for more, that's how far out there I was." "I was sellin' it and usin' it at the same time." He continued, ignoring her last comment. "We decided to go the back way to avoid the cops and the guy that was ridin' next to me lost control of his bike and hit a telephone pole that took his head off, right in front of me."

"Is he makin' this up?" Janice asked Irene.

She shook her head as he continued.

"Blood and brains everywhere and it was one of those unreal scenes that played over and over again in my head but it took that to rock my world." "I thought I was all that and could take anything that the devil had but I was pretty much messed up after that."

"Was this before you were together?"

"We had been married almost a year and I remember callin' mother and tellin' her what had happened." Irene began. "I didn't know what to do because he couldn't eat or sleep for about a week and it was gettin' really bad.

"So what did she say?" Janice asked. "I've heard about how Aunt Frances don't play and I'm half way scared of her."

"She's harmless, believe me." Douglas said. "But when it comes to livin' right she's dead serious and that's the way it should be because your soul is nothin' to play with."

"Yeah, yeah whatever, get back to the story." Janice said with skepticism.

"She told Irene to put me on the phone and all she said were four words that I'll never forget." He said pausing. "She said let God help you and somethin' clicked." "It was a Saturday night and she made us promise to come to church the next day and I told her I would just to get her off my back. He admitted.

"Was this the first time that you had ever been to church or somethin'?" Janice asked, laughing at him.

"I was twenty-five years old and I could probably count on one hand the times that I had been to anybody's church." "But when she told me to let God help me, it did more for me than any drink or reefer ever did and I was into the hard stuff." He continued. "And she didn't judge me or put a guilt trip on me or any of that, even though she probably had the right to."

"How come?"

"Because she felt like he got me off track from the way I was brought up and she was right." Irene began. "I was doin' stuff that probably would've given her a heart attack if she had known about 'em." "But me and my hard headed self didn't care about what she thought." "I was grown."

"But the dude's head out on the street changed all of that huh?"

"It's called comin' to yourself and the Lord knows how to get your attention." "And if that's what it took to wake me up, then that should let you know how self-willed I was." "It was all about what I wanted when I wanted it and nobody could tell me otherwise." Douglas said as he reflected on himself.

"So cut to the chase, what happened after you went to church?" "Did you see this bright light from heaven and all of a sudden you were this changed man?"

"It wasn't a bright light but once I heard about how to get it right, I was obedient to my mother-in-law and let God help me." He said, laughing at himself. "It wasn't complicated or hard to understand and I had enough sense to know that my arms were too short to box with God." He continued as he reflected back in his mind. "That's not original but it's true and when I came up out of that water after they baptized me in the name of Jesus, I felt like I had lost a hundred pounds off my back, I kid you not."

"So that's when you felt like you were this new man huh?"

"That was just the half of it and that's the mistake that a lot of churches make because they stop with baptism." He answered her. "The scripture makes it clear that you have to be born of the water and Spirit and that's where the gift of the Holy Ghost comes in."

"Are you about to get deep with me or somethin'?"

"There's nothin' hard about it but it's just down to earth truth." "Your baptism takes care of whatever you've done in the past and the Holy Ghost is what gives you the power to keep you out of trouble from then on." He said with a knowing emphasis. "It's power that you don't have on your own and because you can't save yourself that's why it's such an awesome thing."

"Then if this what you're tellin' me is such a big deal how come I'm just now hearin' about it?" Janice asked defensively. "Every church I've been to don't talk about this stuff you're sayin' to me and it's all good."

"Nobody is tryin' to take anything away from what you already know but if you don't go all the way with it and do it like scripture says to do it, you just don't have what it takes to make it out of here." Douglas told her. "And the bottom line to all of this is that the Lord is comin' and without this gift that He promised us, we're lost."

"'Nita warned me about you and I should've listened to her because you're tryin' to start somethin' with me." She said after a moment.

"Why would I do that?" "I don't argue about what I know is right because when it happens to you, there's no doubt in your mind that it's truth and you don't have to prove it to anybody."

"It sounds like to me that you're tryin' to prove somethin' that I don't go along with." She started. "I mean I've heard that this church that everybody around here goes to believes in this speakin' in tongues thing and I'm sorry, I can't get with that."

"How come that doesn't surprise me?" He asked her.

"Because you're findin' out that I'm not easy and I don't believe everything that I hear." She said smugly. "I probably go to church just as much as anybody here and I ain't ever spoke in nobody's tongues but that don't mean I'm not just as right as you are." She said, purposely attempting to bait him.

"I have a question for you Janice and you don't have to answer this if you don't want to." Douglas said to her then.

"I can't say if I will or won't."

"Let's try it." He continued. "Let's say that you've been on this job that you really like for four or five years and you're doin' all the right things." "You're never late, you haven't missed any days, the whole nine yards."

"Okay, where are you goin' with this?" She asked him with caution in her voice.

"Just stick with me for a second." "Then one day, your boss calls you into the office and says Janice, you've really been doin' a good job for me." "I appreciate all of your hard work and I think it's time for you to move up in the company." He continued. "We have a position that's open that would pay you another ten grand a year more than what you're makin' now and I think you're qualified for the job." "What do you think your response would be?"

"I'd be crazy not to take it, what do you think?" She threw back at him.

"You just proved my point ma'am."

"How?"

"You said that you would be crazy not to take it and it's not a smart thing to turn down the gift that the Lord promised you just because you don't agree with things that have been proven." He said with a spirit of gentle wisdom." "And nobody here is tryin' to take anything away from what you already know but there's just so much more." "So until you have what God has for you, you just don't have what it takes to make it out of here when the Lord comes."

"I should've listened to 'Nita, you don't play do you?"

"Hon, there's just too much at stake for me to be sugar coatin' anything." Douglas told her. "We're talkin' about eternity and since you brought this up, I don't have a choice but to tell you the truth, no matter how controversial it is."

"Big words, big words." She said, mocking him. "Why can't you talk to me in down to earth words?"

"I'll tell you what ma'am." Douglas began. "I can tell that this isn't goin' anywhere so maybe we just need to leave it like it is because you're startin' to get defensive." "And the last thing I want to do is get you stirred up about this." "It is what it is and that's the end of it.".

CHAPTER 3

FEBRUARY 13, FRIDAY

"This is Friday the thirteenth and since I'm superstitious, I'm watchin' everything and everybody." Janice remarked Friday afternoon at the kitchen table with Ruth, Sheila and Frances.

"Chris told me you were here and I was wonderin' how long it was gonna be before you came to see me." Frances said, as she began snapping green beans in a pot. "I haven't seen you since you were probably seven or eight."

"At the reunion?" Sheila asked.

"All I remember about that was some dry hamburgers and weak kool-aid." Janice said. "I was too young to understand any of all that."

"So who else have you been able to see?"

"I went to see Irene and what's his face, Douglas?" She asked, pretending to forget his name.

"I'm gonna tell him." Sheila said laughing at her. "You called him what's his face."

"What's he gonna do, not a thing." She said with a hint of anger. "And he got on my nerves talkin' about all of that church stuff. She added.

"How did that come up?" Sheila asked.

"I asked him if I could use him as a reference on a job application." She began. "Then I told him that I heard that he had one of them saved from the street stories so I guess it's my fault for bringin' it up."

"You didn't do anything wrong by askin' him about that." Frances told her. "He has a testimony that a lot of people don't have and when he gets half a chance to tell about how the Lord got him out of his mess, he's gonna talk about it."

"Did he tell you about Phillip Mason?" Ruth asked her.

"Is that the dude that got decapitated on the motorcycle?" Janice asked, trying to keep a straight face. "If I had seen that happen, I might've passed out."

"He didn't pass out but when Irene called me to let me know what was goin' on with him, she was almost as bad off as he was." She said as she began to reflect back. "She wasn't used to him havin' a hard time about anything because he was one of those men that was hard as nails and when they were out there runnin' the streets, his nickname was Junkyard."

"Leroy Brown?" Sheila asked starting to laugh with her.

"He was Leroy Brown, meaner than a junkyard dog." She said, shaking her head.

"Who is Leroy Brown?" Janice asked.

"I can probably find it, hold up." Sheila said, picking up her phone.

"Honey there was a song called Bad, Bad Leroy Brown that came out probably about the year you were born so you wouldn't remember it." Frances began. "But it was about this big guy that had everything and thought he was all that." She explained to her. "And one of the lines in the song said that he was meaner than a junkyard dog and that's how Douglas got that nickname."

"Here it is, this is funny." Sheila said as she started playing the lyrics for her from her phone.

"And you know what?" Frances asked two minutes later after they let the song play. "About the only difference in him and Leroy Brown was he didn't have a Eldorado and a Continental but the rest of it pretty much fit him."

"He told me one time that Irene was afraid for you to meet him. Ruth commented.

"She knew better and that's why she was afraid." Frances said. "The first time he came to pick her up, they were headed to the Way Out club over there on the eastside." "And this Negro with these dark glasses and big beard that covered his whole face, walks up to me and says, hey, Douglas Johnson." She continued. "He was high as a kite and comin' to pick my daughter up on a motorcycle and that's all it took for me to start doin' some heavy duty prayin'."

"Where was Uncle William when all of this was goin' on?" Janice asked.

"Honey he's been comin' and goin' for years and I didn't have any choice but to handle things like this by myself."

"How long has he been gone this time?" Sheila asked her.

"He left here maybe fifteen or sixteen years ago, right around the time she started runnin' around with Douglas." She answered as she began opening up to her nieces. "And sometimes I wonder if that had somethin' to do with the way she got together with him."

"Wasn't she in to all of that black power stuff back in the day?" Ruth asked her.

"Big time, she turned against Paul when he married Jane and then when Chris and James got together, she was livid and didn't mind lettin' 'em know how she felt."

"But everybody's one big happy family now huh?" Janice asked with sarcasm in her voice. "Jungle fever and all."

"Everybody still has their own set of problems but compared to the way those two were and the way they are now, it's like night and day." Frances said. "There's nothin' too hard for God and that's who it takes to turn people's lives around; and to show you how the Lord works, Douglas was the one to get the Holy Ghost before she did and that was the start of the trouble in that camp."

"Yeah that's not the way it usually happens." Sheila commented "She was brought up around church and all of that and he didn't know anything about this."

"But God knows the hearts of every one of us and he might've acted like Leroy Brown but He saw somethin' in him that He could use and He knows how to draw you like nothin' or nobody else can." Frances said. "The night that he came home from church with the Holy Ghost, Irene told me that he went in to their liquor cabinet and poured twenty some bottles of booze down the toilet and that's when she knew that he meant business."

"Twenty bottles?" Ruth asked, surprised.

"You heard me right and she knew that that was the end of their night clubs and partyin' and whatever else they were used to doin' and it was tearin' her up." Frances said, remembering. "And when it got to the place where she was ready to leave him, Paul sat her down and talked some sense into her but it was close to a year before she realized that he wasn't playin' church."

"She told me herself how much she put him through and when she saw that he wasn't goin' back to the way he was, she just sort of gave up." Sheila remarked.

"So he just quit the drugs and all that cold turkey?" Janice asked with icy skepticism.

"He never smoked another joint or cigarette, his potty mouth went away and so on and so on because the Holy Ghost is powerful." Frances answered her. "And the next time you get a chance to talk to him, he'll tell you himself how much he got delivered from."

"I'm not goin' there with him anymore, I think I've heard enough to know what he's about and if that's what's gettin' him through the night, more power to him." She said irritably.

"How come nobody invited me to the party?" Paul said then as he walked in the side door."

"Did you come to see me?" Janice asked him.

"I heard that you were in town sort of sudden like." He said after giving Frances a hug and sitting down next to her.

"News travels fast huh?"

"Pretty much." "How long are you gonna be here?"

"I bought a one-way plane ticket, read between the lines." Janice told him, half-way joking.

"Havin' a bad day hon?" He asked her.

"Everybody is havin' a bad day, it's Friday the thirteenth."

"Jane's mother called her today and you're probably not gonna believe what she told her." He said as he intentionally ignored her last comment.

"We don't need any bad news, what's goin' on?" Frances asked him.

"She said she was tired of seein' her grandkids livin' in a cracker box so she called a realtor and bought a four acre lot for us to build a bigger house on."

"What?" Sheila asked, in shock.

"You heard me." "She was cryin' when she called me at school and I thought somethin' had happened to one of the kids."

"So where is this lot?"

"We haven't seen it yet but she told me that it's ten miles from where we are now, off of two thirty-five."

"Wait a minute, back up." Janice said suddenly. "This is your mother-in-law that's doin' this for you just because she can?"

"No strings attached; she has it like that and for a minute, I thought about tellin' Jane to tell her that we can't let her do that." He began.

"But you couldn't let pride get in the way of the blessin' that the Lord has for you." Frances said, finishing his thought. "And if you had done that, you might've gotten a good workin' over from me because I'm your mother and I can do that."

"Wait another minute, I'm not finished askin' you some questions about this." Janice said again. "Is this woman a millionaire or somethin'?"

"Jane's father was a C.E.O. for a pharmaceutical company before he died a couple of years ago." He started. "And when we got married, he pretty much didn't want anything else to do with her and I'm thinkin' that this is her way of makin' it up to her." He said thoughtfully.

"So what are you gonna do with four acres of land, that's a lot to take care of." Ruth commented.

I'm gettin' to that, hold up." "I sent James a text and told him that I need to talk to him." He said, checking his phone for a response from him.

"Are you gonna have him do your blueprints and all of that?" Sheila asked him. "That is so exciting, I'm about to cry like Jane."

"We've been talkin' about findin' a bigger place but we haven't said anything to anybody else about it." He said.

"Honey you know that God is a provider and He knows how to put things on the hearts of people so now you have another testimony." Frances told him.

"When 'Nita told me how many kids you have I thought she was lyin.'" Janice told him. "What's with the nineteen kids?"

"It's personal, don't lose any sleep over it."

"I mean I thought Chris and James were insane for havin' seven but you got twice as many." She persisted. "What's up with that, seriously?" "Don't the drug stores around here sell birth control?"

"Janice you are crazy, leave it alone." Sheila told her, trying hard not to laugh at the last comment from her

"Saved by the bell." She said as his phone rang.

"What's so funny about that?" She asked as Paul got up to answer the call. "I mean all of these kids around here are makin' me dizzy, I'm not kiddin." She added. "I didn't know that I had so many little cousins and most of 'em are bi." "I'm tryin' to be nice but it's not easy."

"It just happened that way and after you've been here awhile, you won't even notice it." Frances told her.

"I already noticed that about James, Chris rubbed off on him big time."

"Have you thought about doin' some babysittin' 'til you find a job honey?" Frances asked her.

"Just in case somebody wants a date night or somethin'?" She asked after a moment. "If I do, I'm gonna start out with Paul, I have to see that to believe it."

"I heard that." He said coming back in." "You wanna take a ride?"

"That depends on where we're goin."

"James is comin' by when he gets off work so you can just ride back home with him when we get done." He told her. "How did you get over here anyway?"

"I called Sheila and told her to come and pick me up so I could see Aunt Frances, I'm makin' my rounds so I might as well go check out that nursery school you have." She said, getting up. "I need to see this for myself."

"So in other words, you need to know if there's enough land out there for two three thousand square foot houses." James asked an hour later, taking notes on a pad.

"That depends on what Chris has to say about that, do you think she'd be willin' to move that far out?"

"There's just one way to find out but I think I could probably talk her into it." He said after a moment. "The only thing about that is sellin' the place where we are and that might take awhile."

"How do you feel about that leavin' that house?" Paul asked him cautiously.

"I would have to get used to the idea but this is a chance that we really can't pass up Paul and we really don't know how to thank-you."

"Her mother did this for us and it's really more than we need so why not?" "She blessed us so we're blessin' you and this is family." He continued. "Sounds a little mushy but whatever it takes, go for it."

"Then what about doin' it this way?" James began. "What if I get your blueprints drawn up at no charge, and I might be crazy for thinkin' this but we could probably get enough people together from church to actually build it." He continued. "That way, you would just have to buy the materials and wouldn't have to worry about labor costs."

"That's a little idealistic but if we could get it to work, it would be like the icin' on the cake, no kiddin'."

"My take on it is that there's a need; your kids are not gettin' any smaller and mine aren't either and since the Lord moved on your mother-in-law like this, it's up to us to do the rest." James said. "Plain and simple."

"So where do we go from here?"

"I'm gonna go home and lay it all out to Chris and I have a feelin' that she won't turn this down." He said. "Then you and Jane need to decide how you want your house to be laid out and I'll get the blueprints done."

"We need to take a trip out there and actually see what we're workin' with so whenever you get the time, let me know."

"When I walked in the door I was expectin' to see kids runnin' all over the place, where are they?" Janice asked, talking with Jane as she was folding laundry in the kitchen.

"They're all upstairs and they know that they can't be runnin' all over the place, Paul would have a fit."

"I can tell that he don't play but I guess that comes from bein' the principal huh?"

"Exactly, they're afraid of him and if you get sent to his office, you can count on gettin' expelled for a couple of days."

"You don't look like you've had so many kids, what's up with that?' Janice asked boldly.

"Thanks for the compliment but I just work it off."

"So your mother just decided to do this for you for no reason?" She asked, purposely changing the subject. "Paul said she did it to make up for some stuff." She added while attempting to stir up trouble.

"He might be right about that because for awhile, she pretty much disowned me because I went totally opposite from what she had planned for me." She said, laughing a little. "I was her only kid and my parents sent me to college thinkin' that I was gonna be somethin' they could brag about, but when it went the other way, it was some trouble in the camp, big time." She added, thinking back.

"Where did you meet Paul?"

"This is how it went down." She began. "Have you met James' sister Lynn yet?"

She shook her head.

"We were dorm roommates her freshman year and that Christmas she invited me to come here with her for break."

"How come you didn't go home?"

"They were in Europe somewhere and Lynn didn't want me to be myself for two weeks." She explained.

"So you just hit it off right away huh?"

"Yeah we were kind of close but because she wasn't involved in a lot of campus stuff-

"Because she was always goin' to church, right?" Janice interrupted.

"It went deeper than church and she never did try to force anything on me or act like she was better than anybody else but I started watchin' her." Jane continued. "I had a lot of friends that went to church all the time but it was somethin' different about her, and it got my attention and that's when she started to tell me about the Holy Ghost."

"What does all of that have to do with Paul?" Janice asked, determined to turn the conversation in another direction. "Did you meet at church?"

"We did and the rest is history as they say and my parents didn't want anything to do with us." "But when my father died a couple of years ago, she got everything that he had in stocks and C.D.s and all of that so she won't even feel this."

"So this is her peace offerin' for the way she acted?"

"Maybe so, I was too shocked to ask her that but whatever it was, it was right on time." Jane said. "So who else have you been able to see since you got here?"

"I went to Irene's house the other day and Sheila picked me up so I could see Aunt Frances." "She told me that I could probably start babysittin' 'til I find a job somewhere."

"That makes sense, that way you would get to know all forty-one of 'em." Jane commented

"Is that how many grandkids Aunt Frances has?" Janice asked.

She nodded. "And Donna is due in May so it never really stops." She added. "But I don't think that we're gonna do that anymore, it's time to let somebody else take over."...

Chapter 4

March 11, Wednesday

"We told Janice that we'd be back in an hour so we need to do this pretty fast." Paul remarked at the dining room table with Chris and James, three weeks later.

"Gotcha, we don't need to rock that boat." James said as he opened up the blueprints for their house.

"Paul this is huge, are you sure you want all of this?" Chris asked him.

"By the time we get furniture and kids in here, it's not gonna seem as big and they need to be separated a little bit because they're startin' to get on each other's nerves, you know what I mean?" Jane said.

"They're growin' up and you're gonna be glad that you have this much room once we get it up. James said. "This is your entrance facin' south, you have two rooms, one on the east of the entry way and one on the west and the room dimensions are identical."

"What does that say, sixteen by ten apiece?" Jane asked, leaning over to read the numbers.

"Will that be big enough or do you want it bigger than that?" James asked them.

"These two rooms are gonna be like play rooms, one for ten and under and the other one for the older ones so that sounds big enough."

"And you're doin' the open concept thing here for your dining area and kitchen, right?" He asked, as he "walked" them through the print.

"You got it, the only walls we need are gonna be between bedrooms and bathrooms." Paul said.

"And there's four bedrooms and one bathroom on each of these hallways?" Chris asked.

"There's eight bedrooms, two oversized bathrooms, sort of dorm style and the master suite, that's over here next to the kitchen." James said. "That won't be a problem will it?"

"I don't know why it would be, this looks like what we had in mind so let's go for it." Paul told him.

"Have you got your house on the market yet?" Chris asked.

"Not for a couple of months because if we sell before this one is ready, we've got a big problem." Paul said.

"If we can break ground when the weather warms up, it'll take probably three to four months to do this." James started. "I'm gonna get a brotherhood meetin' together in a couple of weeks so we can get organized because this is a major project."

"When are you gonna have time to supervise this, are you sure you wanna do this James?" Jane asked him.

"Don't have a choice ma'am." "I wouldn't have started this if I wasn't gonna finish it and since we're goin' out there too, that's more reason to get this done."

"This should let you know how desperate I am because I just left Paul and Jane's house from watchin' their kids and now it's your turn." Janice remarked after Irene let her in around eight-thirty. "And I am spendin' the night, right?"

"Yeah, I have to be at the kid's school to talk to a couple of teachers at nine 'o clock so I'll make sure that they eat breakfast and all of that stuff before I leave."

"What did everybody do for babysitters before I hit town, I've been all over the place changin' diapers and watchin' cartoons."

"I don't know but we're glad that you're available." Irene said as she took her coat.

"Is Mr. Douglas here?"

"Mr. Douglas Janice?" Irene said, laughing at her. "If he heard you callin' him that, he'd get you straight in a second." "He's up there in the kitchen, go on up, he won't bite you." She added as she started back towards the basement.

"I thought that was you down there, what's up ma'am?" He asked her a minute later as he put work information on a laptop.

"I still need a job, I've been here three weeks and nothin's happenin.'" She said as she sat down at the table across from him.

"I heard that you've been doin' some heavy duty babysittin', that's a job." He said as he began to give her his full attention.

"I can't do that forever and everywhere I go I end up hearin' somebody talk about church and God and all that." She said irritably. "One of Chris' kids ended up tellin' me about the three guys that got put in the furnace and how God didn't let 'em get burned up." She continued. "I mean give me a break."

"How did that come up?" Douglas asked her, amused.

"James made a fire in the fireplace the other day and I think it was Patty that asked me if I knew about that story in the bible where God helped those three dudes in the furnace that didn't get burned up." She repeated. "I don't need kids tellin' me stuff like I've never been to church before."

"Are you gettin' stuff off your chest?"

"Can you tell?" She asked him. "Then one other day, and this really ticked me off." She said, thinking a moment. "One of 'em told me that God was everywhere and if I did bad things that I was gonna be in trouble."

"You have to remember that these are kids talkin' and sometimes they don't really know what they're sayin." Douglas told her. "But on the other hand, which ever one 'em said it had a point, even though it might've sounded kind of rough." He added.

"It's like I can't get away from it; and maybe I made a mistake by comin' here in the first place."

"No you didn't because you're around people that love you and it might seem like things are workin' against you but it'll all come together." He said, reassuring her.

"Douglas don't start tellin' me a bunch of good soundin' words because I've heard all of that before and it just seems to never work for me."

"Are you stressin' out because you haven't found a job yet?" "Is that your biggest thing?"

"Don't you think that's enough?" She threw at him as she continued to vent.

"I've been where you are so don't think that this is somethin' new." He calmly told her with genuine empathy. "And what you need to do is settle down about it because you're makin' yourself feel worse."

"You don't really know how I'm feelin' because you're on another level,-

"Hold up, don't go there." He interrupted her. "Back up off of that one." He told her.

"But that's the way I feel, it's like I'm the only one around here that's not into the church thing and I'm sorry, that's not what I'm about right now."

"Okay, I'm gonna back you up a second." He answered her. "It's not the church thing that you're against, it's all of a sudden you're around people that have the Spirit of God and you don't quite know how to react to that." He added.

She didn't answer but avoided eye contact with him as she wiped tears from her face.

"And there's somethin' else goin' on with you isn't it?" He asked as he handed her a napkin.

"I'm pregnant Douglas." She finally spoke after a long moment as she let more tears freely fall." "And I am so scared."

He didn't respond but allowed her to continue talking, under the direction of the Holy Ghost as he began to experience an overwhelming sense of being touched with the feelings of her situation.

"When I first found out, I wanted to get an abortion but I couldn't get the money together." She barely said. "And then when I told my mother, they told me that I wouldn't be able to stay there because it wouldn't look right for a deacon's daughter to be knocked up, and that's just the way she said it." She finished, nearly hysterical.

"Janice hold on honey, this will be okay." Douglas told her as he wiped his face with a handkerchief.

"Janice what's goin' on honey?" Irene asked as she came in after overhearing her from the basement. "What happened?" She asked him as she put an arm around her to calm her shaking.

"Pregnant." He said in a matter of fact way.

"Is that why you left D.C.?" She asked her.

She nodded a little. "I didn't know where else to go and I really didn't mean for this to come off like this." She added, still trying to calm herself. "It's because of what she said that I didn't want anything to do with anybody's church." She said, explaining her behavior.

"How far are you Janice?" Douglas asked her.

"I'm probably about eight or nine weeks." She said after thinking a moment. "And how did you know?" She asked him.

"I could tell that you were holdin' somethin' back and whatever you do, don't be sorry that you didn't get an abortion."

"Why?" "If I had, I wouldn't be in this mess." She said.

"Your baby is not a mess and we'll help you get through this so stop stressin' out Janice." Irene told her. "Have you told anybody else?"

She shook her head. "And I'm scared to tell James and Chris because they should've known about it when I first got here."

"You don't have any reason to be scared about that, what do you think they're gonna do, put you out on the street?" Douglas asked her.

"Maybe that's what needs to happen." She said wearily.

"Stop beatin' up on yourself." He gently told her. "It happened, and there's nothin' you can do but go forward with it."

"It's not too late-

"'Fraid so ma'am, that's not an option." He said, interrupting her. "And I'm gonna ask you a question and I want you to promise me that I'll get an honest answer from you."

"Okay, maybe." She said shrugging.

"If you had really wanted to do that, do you think you would've come out with it like you just did?" He asked her. "Truth time."

"Maybe not, I don't know." She said after a moment as Irene sat a cup of tea in front of her.

"You wouldn't have and you let us know because you need help with this and there's nothin' wrong with that."

"Okay junkyard." She said as she tried to smile.

"Somebody's been talkin' to you but that's okay too." He said, amused. "That just helps me to stay thankful for how the Lord got me out of trouble."

"Don't you feel better since we know now?" Irene asked her.

"I do but I still need to talk to Chris and James as soon as I can." She said. "And now I wish I had told 'em when I first got here but that would've been a lot of nerve."

"Because?" Douglas asked her.

"They didn't even know I was comin' 'til I called from the airport." She explained. "I told 'Nita but she didn't believe me with her crazy self and how wacked out would that be to say, by the way, I'm pregnant, get over it." "And I didn't know they had seven kids 'til it was too late so I'm just makin' it worse for them."

"One thing at a time." Douglas told her as he called their number.

"Don't go anywhere." Janice nervously told Irene as she struggled to keep her composure.

"Hey Chris have you got a minute or two?" Douglas asked her as he got up to leave the room after she answered the phone.

"Yeah, what's goin' on, you don't sound like yourself."

"Janice just told us that she's pregnant and it's been a little emotional over here tonight."

"Is she okay?" Chris asked after a moment as she felt her own emotions start to surface.

"She will be but it might be awhile before she gets over some stuff." He began. "She told Roy and Kathryn when she first found out and they gave her this line about not bein' able to stay there because he's a deacon and she would make him look bad."

"Are you kiddin' me Douglas?"

"You heard me right but that's beside the point right now."

"Wait a minute, that's not beside the point." She said, disagreeing with him. "How self-righteous and ugly is that?"

"Chris calm down, hear me out." He told her. "I had the same thoughts myself but does it really matter what we think?" "What they did or didn't do is not up to us to judge."

"Douglas-

"I know that you don't have a lot of patience with things like this but it is what it is and right now, she's worried about how you and James are gonna react." He continued. "Is he there?"

"He's here but let me talk to her first."

"Chris I'm sorry, I really didn't mean for this to happen." Janice told her over the phone a few minutes later.

"We know honey but why were you afraid to tell us?" Chris asked her.

"Maybe I was in some kind of denial or somethin'." She said after a moment. "And I think I was afraid the same thing would happen here that went on at home." She added. "Does James know yet?"

"Yeah he knows and the sky didn't fall did it?" James asked her.

She didn't answer as a feeling of relief overwhelmed her to the point of near collapse."

"Janice listen to me for a minute." James told her. "Nothin' has changed so you don't have to worry about findin' somewhere else to live." He said, reassuring her. "And we just decided to move out to the country with Paul and Jane so if you're worried about crowdin' us out, that's not an issue."

"And even if we weren't movin', it would still be the same thing so just relax about it for a minute Janice, you'll get through this." Chris told her. "We love you and your baby too so it's all good.".

MARCH 14, SATURDAY

"James and Chris and Paul went out to the lot to take pictures and Sheila told me that you wanted to talk to me so they dropped me off." Janice told Frances Saturday afternoon as she took her coat off and laid it on the sofa.

"Are you feelin' alright?"

She nodded a little. "So I guess it's out huh?" She asked as she sat down.

"That's the way it happens with families honey."

"You're not gonna preach to me are you?" She asked as she noticed her bible on the coffee table.

"That's not what I do, I'm just a little concerned about you and your mother." She answered. "I don't like to see this kind of stuff goin' on because you never know when somethin' might happen."

"I wasn't the one that turned on her, it was the other way around Aunt Frances." Janice said. "All they could talk about was how people were gonna be talkin' about the head deacon's daughter and I took the hint and left."

"Have you talked to her since you got here?"

She shook her head. "I talked to Marie a couple of weeks ago and she told me that she was stayin' out of it."

"Because she's your sister and she doesn't want to be in the middle of you two but somethin' has to give sweetheart, this can't go on like this."

"I might talk to her but she can't make me go back to D.C." She said with determination.

"Is that because you feel comfortable here now?" Frances asked her.

"I do and just about everybody else moved away so now it's my turn." She said. "And I might have a job too so I have to be where I can make some money for this baby."

"Has somethin' come through for you?"

"James told me the other day that one of the secretaries in his office just put in her two weeks notice so that might work out." She said. "And it's who you know, not what you know."

"That's true too and we know that things will work themselves out but don't forget about your mother and father." "You have your differences but they're still your parents." Frances admonished her. "And when your father and me were growin' up together, he would do mean things on purpose just to see how much he could get away with but he would always come back and apologize."

She nodded a little before speaking. "Whatever, but he was as serious as a heart attack when he told me to get my stuff together and make arrangements somewhere else and that's when I called 'Nita and told her that I was comin'."

"But you know what honey, you need to be really thankful that you had somewhere to come because it could've been a lot different."

"I am but I still feel sort of bad about the other night when I was talkin' to Douglas." She began. "I don't understand how he knew that this was goin' on when I hadn't told anybody and then after he got it out of me, he was sittin' there wipin' tears just like I was.

"Was that the first time you had seen a man cry?"

"It was and he wasn't tryin' to hide it or anything and I'm sittin' there trippin'." "How did he know what was goin' on?" She asked her again.

"That's somethin' that you're gonna have to ask him but I do know this." She began. "When you have the spirit of God, sometimes He will let you know certain things about people and that's what the scripture calls the Word of Knowledge." She concluded.

"That's scary."

"Honey he's harmless and he might have wanted you to see that he's concerned about you and he's willin' to do whatever he can to help you."

"But it's just hard to trust somebody that you just met, I've only known him and James for a little over a month."

"They know that and they don't expect you to be anything else than what you are." "It'll take some time for you to see what they're really about."

"What are they about though Aunt Frances?" She asked with sincerity as she felt herself opening up to her. "I really do wanna believe what I see but I'm scared to." She admitted.

"What are you seeing?"

"I mean how is James so laid back about everything?" She asked. "He's just the opposite from Chris and I guess that's why they work together." She said, allowing herself to laugh a little.

29

"They're crazy about each other but they've been through some serious issues because of obvious reasons but when couples let the Lord handle things, you can't help but make it."

"Is that what it is?"

"That has a lot to do with it because I remember how hard it was for them when they first got married." "Irene had a stroke and so did his people but because they were determined to stay right with God, they overcame a lot of ugly stuff."

"Irene didn't like it?" She asked, shocked.

"She was really in to the black power thing that was goin' on right around the time they got married and of course this was before she got the Holy Ghost." Frances said, pausing. "This was right before her and Douglas got together and it was the oddest thing, as hard as a rock as he was, he never went there with her."

"That's crazy."

"To you and me it is but God looks on the hearts of people and evidently, He saw somethin' in him that nobody else did." She continued. "He was junkyard to everybody that knew him but when He got ready to save him from all of that, He knew just how to do it because He's God and all souls belong to Him." She stressed as she began to rejoice at her own words.

"The guy on the motorcycle?" Janice asked quietly.

"Phillip Mason was his name and Douglas told me later on that he almost put a gun to his head because he couldn't get that scene out of his mind."

"He said there was blood and brains everywhere." Janice said, remembering his testimony.

"But because God hears and answers prayer is probably the reason that He didn't allow the devil to take him out." Frances said. "I had never prayed so much in my life as I did when they were out there and it took awhile, but when He did it, it was an awesome thing to see."

"Wow."

"So don't be afraid to trust what you see from him and James and I wouldn't be tellin' you that if I didn't know for myself what the power of God can do." Frances told her in a spirit of love and concern.

"Douglas told me the other night after I talked to them that if I needed to talk some more that I could call him but I don't know if I should do that yet."

"He probably told you that because you trusted him enough to tell him what was goin' on in the first place." Frances told her. "And if you're worried about some funny stuff goin' on, that's not gonna happen." She reassured her. "He's old enough to be your father so we're not goin' there."

"Maybe that's what it was, it was somethin' about the way he got down on my level, you know what I mean?"

"And you've never gotten that at home?"

She shook her head. "No way, he never let me talk to him about any of my problems or if I wanted to know somethin' about guys or any of that, he just wasn't there." She added. "And that's probably why I'm knocked up right now."

"Did you get the chance to tell the baby's father?"

"I told him right after I found out, then he told me that it was my problem and he hung up on me."

"So he's probably not willin' to help you with child support or anything like that?"

"No way, I'm on my own." "And after I found out that he wasn't gonna have anything to do with it, I almost went to one of those clinics and took care of it that way and I still can." She said in a matter of fact way. "It's not too late."

"And how do you think you'd feel if you went through with that?" Frances asked her after a moment.

"I don't know, I'm just kiddin.'" She said, shrugging. "Douglas told me that wasn't an option so I guess I can't".

CHAPTER 5

MARCH 16, MONDAY

"The pizzas are gonna be here in ten minutes Jimmy, get your funds together." 'Nita told James Monday night as she passed out Monopoly money at the kitchen table. "And since we're on spring break, get ready for a long, crazy night so don't try to get out of goin' bankrupt."

"Says you 'Nita Scott." "You don't scare me."

"I'm gonna buy all of the railroads and beat everybody." Patty remarked as she put cards on the board.

"Janice are you playin'?" 'Nita asked her as she filled the dishwasher.

"Not this time, I'm goin' to bed in a few minutes." She said irritably.

"It's too early to be goin' to bed, we need one more player, the more the merrier." 'Nita told her as Chris came in with the phone and handed it to Janice.

"Who is it?" She asked cautiously.

"Your mommy." She said. "It'll be okay, trust me."

"We talked about it and decided that we can work somethin' out for you here instead of you imposin' on Chris' family like you are." Kathryn told her a few minutes later as she sat in the living room alone.

"I've already made up my mind to stay here, that would be too much trouble for me to go through all that again."

"What kind of trouble?" "If you need money for a plane ticket, that's not a problem honey." She insisted.

"For one thing, I just got a job that I'm startin' in a couple of weeks and I would just rather be here."

"Do they know that you're pregnant?" She asked as she became increasingly impatient with her.

"I told them last week about that so you don't have any reason to worry about me anymore."

"So you were there for a whole month before you let them know what was goin' on'?" She threw at her. "And just like that, they're lettin' you stay there with no strings attached?" "Don't be so silly and gullible girl."

"Do we have to keep talkin' about this?" Janice asked, trying to stay calm with her.

"I think we need to talk about you gettin' on a plane and actin' like you have some sense." "And just because you're eighteen years old does not mean that you know how to handle things like this by yourself."

"What would change if I decided to come back?" Janice asked after a moment. "I don't need you to always be remindin' me about this and if you don't leave me alone about it, I know how to really take care of it and it's not too late." She said as she slammed the phone down.

"Is everything okay?" James asked her as he walked in from the kitchen.

"I just hung up on my mother and right now I don't care." She managed to say as he sat down. "And I'm tryin' to do the right thing but she just called and set me back."

"How do you mean set you back?"

"I'm really tryin' to wrap my head around it and I know that it's not a big deal to anybody but me and she just made it seem like it was the end of the world." She answered him. "And this is exactly why I don't need to talk to her at all right now."

"When you said that it reminded me of how my mother turned on me because of Chris." He began. "And we were older than you are but by the time she got done workin' me over, it was like I was ten or eleven years old."

"Just because Chris is not white?"

"That's exactly it and it was so bizarre because it was so sudden, it came out of nowhere."

"How did it come up?"

"She would always have us over for dinner on Christmas Eve, it was a pitch-in kind of deal and I called and asked her what she wanted us to bring." He began. "Then she told me that I needed to come by myself and I'm like, excuse me?"

"So how did she let you know that was the reason?"

"She wouldn't come out and say it because she knew that I would go all the way off and if it hadn't been for the Lord helpin' me, it would've been a seriously bad day in here."

"What were you gonna do, tell her off or somethin'?"

"I wouldn't have gone that far because I would've had to go back and apologize to her even though she was the one that was wrong." He said, thinking back to the incident. "Chris was about seven months pregnant with Stephen and I really didn't want her to get in the middle of it but she could tell that somethin' was goin' on and I didn't have a choice but to tell her."

"Was she mad or upset about it?"

"It got to her at first but she's a lot different now and she made both of us grow some pretty thick skin when it comes to that."

"Did you get stuff straightened out before she died?" Janice asked as she began to forget about her phone conversation.

"Neither one of us brought it back up again but after she let me know what she thought about me marryin' Chris, somethin' sort of drained out of me and it never came back." He replied. "Sounds a little dramatic or corny but it's true anyhow."

"It's startin' to feel that way with me and if she don't lay off of me, I might do somethin' crazy."

"Did you tell her that you're goin' to work in a couple of weeks?"

"Yeah I told her but that didn't make her any difference, all she could talk about was how I need to come back home because I'm gettin' in the way here."

"Maybe I need to talk to her."

"Don't waste your time James, she's too busy thinkin' that she's gonna control me but that's not happenin.'" "And they blew it way back in January when I first told 'em everything and all they were worried about was how I was gonna make them look at church so I'm done with them for right now."

"Maybe you just need to sleep on it, give it some time." James told her as he went to answer the door. "Eat a couple of pieces of pizza and forget about it for a minute.".

MARCH 20, FRIDAY

"You didn't waste any time comin' over here did you?" Frances asked after Douglas came in the back door Friday afternoon.

"I was about to leave work anyway and your voicemail sounded too serious for me to wait." "What's goin on?" He asked as he sat down across from her at the breakfast nook in the kitchen.

"Kathryn called me about six-thirty this mornin' and I thought somebody had died, I'm not kiddin' you." She said as she closed the newspaper in front of her.

He didn't comment but proceeded to silence his phone so as not to be interrupted.

"She called to let me know that she'll be here around this time tomorrow and she'll be takin' Janice back with her after she gives you a piece of her mind as she put it."

"Let me get this straight before I say another word because I see where this is goin'." He said calmly.

"Janice has no idea what she has in mind and this is gonna get real ugly, believe me when I tell you."

"It doesn't have to be, don't think too far ahead of yourself." He told her. "But back up a minute, how did I get in the mix?"

"Honey you are one of the main ingredients in this cake that's in the works so put your seat belt on." She said with a straight face. "It was you that was the first to find out what was goin' on with her and you're probably the one that's gonna have the most influence on her and she's havin' a hard time with that."

"Have you talked to Roy about this at all?"

"Roy Scott is in another world, he's probably too busy bein' the head deacon to care about what's goin' on with his daughter and believe me when I tell you, he has done some major damage." Frances said with a knowing tone in her voice. "And the only reason she knows anything about you is because of what I had to tell her." "I had to let her know what happened because I had to prepare her for what Janice is probably gonna tell her and I can just imagine what that conversation will be like."

"Have you talked to her since that night?"

"She was over here about a week ago and we got an understandin' about some things." She began. "She needs to know that this is a family and what affects one affects all of us, and it doesn't matter how sensitive it might be, she can't handle all of this by herself."

"All of that's true but the last thing I want to do is give Kathryn or Janice or anybody else for that matter the impression that I'm tryin' to take the place of her father, I can't go there." He said with God given wisdom.

"Of course you can't, that would do more harm than good but when you put yourself out there like you did, it pretty much made an impression on her that she's not gonna be able to forget for a long time." Frances told him. "And I know that you've been around the block more times than any of us ever have but I'm tellin' you again to let God help you."

"I'm listenin' to everything that you're tellin' me but that's a fine line that I can't cross and believe me, when she dropped that bomb on me, it was like it was one of my own girls and I can't really explain it but there it is." He admitted.

"I think you know what it was Douglas and the Lord knows how much she's gone through, even before she got here, and if He chooses to use you to fill in some gaps, don't be surprised."

"So tell me this, what makes her think that she's gonna be able to make her go back to D. C. with her?" He asked her after a moment.

"She's not dealin' with a twelve or thirteen year old kid and she should know Janice better than that by now." "She is not a push over, I could tell that the first time I talked to her."

"And I'm not so sure that that's not a defense mechanism of hers because when I was talkin' to her last week, I saw a side of her that was just like a baby but she's not gonna let everybody see that." Frances said. "If she lets her guard down it's because you have her trust and as far as Kathryn goes, get ready for some venom."

"Who's pickin' her up at the airport?"

"Sheila said she would and she's takin' her to Chris and James' so she can see Janice but I don't know how she's plannin' to corner you."

"If she's really determined to talk to me, I'm all ears but she's not gonna be able to intimidate me." He said. "But thanks for the warnin' and I'll let you know how it goes."

MARCH 21, SATURDAY

"I need to sit down with Chris and her husband before I deal with Janice and whether she realizes it or not, she can't move in on them and expect everything to be okay." Kathryn remarked Saturday as she and Sheila waited at the luggage carousel for her bags.

"Does she know that you're here?"

"I asked Frances to let them know and I hope that she did but it doesn't matter because I'm here and all of this is about to change." She said with determination. "And maybe you need to call them to make sure they know that "I'm on my way."

"She went to the store with Chris, they should be back in a minute." James said half an hour later after sitting down in the living room with Kathryn and Sheila. "But they know you're here, I just sent Chris a text message." He added.

"If you need me to get lost I can because I'm not really involved in this am I?" Sheila asked, nudging James.

"I'm leavin' that up to you but don't leave yet, I need you to call Irene's husband, what's his name?" Kathryn asked.

"Douglas." She said.

"I need to have a conversation with him too because I need to get a lot of things off of my chest and we're endin' all of this mess tonight."

"Just have him come over here if he can because we need to get all of this out in the open." James spoke up. "Enough is enough."

"I'll call him." Sheila said as she got up and went towards the kitchen, glad for a reason to leave the room.

"So what's the issue, are you thinkin' that havin' Janice here is a problem or is it that you want her back in D.C.?" James asked her.

"It's a combination of both things and I appreciate you and Chris for lettin' her stay here but she needs to be at home."

"It hasn't been a problem and the last time I talked to her about it, she wasn't interested in goin' back." James replied as he heard Chris and Janice come in the back door.

"Is that them?" She asked as she started to get up.

"I tried to get back before you got here but the lines got long." Chris said as Kathryn approached them.

"It's okay, I was just in there talkin' to James." She said, waiting on Janice to react to her presence. "Honey don't I get a hug?" She asked her.

She nodded a little as she gave her a quick embrace.

"Are you feelin' okay?"

"I guess I do, I don't know how I'm supposed to feel." She said with an indifferent tone. She said as she started to help Chris with the groceries.

"Did you need to talk to her by yourself?' Chris asked as she sensed the tension between them.

"Go ahead and finish what you're doin', I'm still talkin' to James in here." She said, going back into the living room.

"Douglas is on his way, he said give him fifteen minutes." Sheila announced then. "I'll be upstairs with 'Nita, I'm gettin' out of the way."

"Before you came in a few minutes ago I was tellin' James that I appreciate how you two have let Janice stay here for the last couple of months but she really does need to come back home." Kathryn remarked a few minutes later after Chris came in and sat on the sofa next to him.

"But don't you think that's up to her?" Chris asked.

"Hold up a second, I don't think we have any business talkin' about her and around her when she's right here in the house and can talk for herself." James spoke up then. "Do you have anything against her bein' in here?" He asked Kathryn.

"I would like for her to be in here but a few minutes ago, she acted like she didn't wanna be bothered and that's not her." "What in the world have you been tellin' her about me that's made her act like I'm a total stranger?" She insisted.

"We haven't been tellin' her anything, that's not what we're here for." Chris quickly came back. "Why would we do that?"

"Somebody has and I can get it out of her if you don't want to tell me, I promise you." "I know her better than anybody and this is exactly why she needs to come on back home where she belongs." She added as Janice walked in.

"I don't think so." "You just wasted your time and money comin' out here 'cause I'm not goin' back with you." Janice said with determination. "Sorry." She added with sarcasm.

"Don't you think this house is full enough already?" "They don't need you and another baby to complicate things so you just need to face the facts here, as much as you don't want to admit it."

"How do you know how full this house is, this is the first time you've ever been in here." She came back. "And that's not even the point." Janice said trying to control her emotions.

"Then what's the point Janice?" "This is the reason that I got busy and came out here to get to the bottom of things so if you need to yell and scream and do whatever it is you do, go right ahead because this is the time to do it." Kathryn said after Douglas walked in the front door. "Are you Douglas?" She asked as she became increasingly angry.

"Yes ma'am, are you Kathryn?" He asked her after a moment as he looked past her while taking note of Janice's deterioration on the other side of the room. "Chris." He added as he motioned her to remove her.

"Excuse me, I was talkin' to her." Kathryn told him half a minute later.

"You were talkin' at her, not to her and I came over here because I was told that you need to talk to me." He said as he sat down.

"I need to talk to you because I heard that you were the first one that she confided in about the mess she got herself in and that just doesn't seem right to me." "She barely knows you so how did you manage to get her trust like that so fast?"

"I haven't had the chance to ask her that but I will tell you this." He began. "Anytime that the Lord puts somebody in front of me like she was that night, I don't have a choice but to see them the same way that He does. "And it was just a matter of listenin' to what she had to say and out it came."

"But you don't know her like that." She said interrupting him.

"I don't have to know you but all souls belong to God and if I had decided to be on some kind of self-righteous trip, she might've hidden it 'til she couldn't anymore." He continued. "She was afraid to tell James and Chris because she thought she'd get the same reaction that she did at home and a person can only take so much before there's a breakin' point."

"What do you mean a breakin' point?" Kathryn threw at him. "She brought this on herself and it looks like to me that everybody here is makin' her feel like everything is gonna be alright." She continued with a spirit of indignation.

"Nobody has told her that but she does need to know that she won't be goin' through it by herself." Douglas told her.

"So what's in this for you?" "I wasn't born yesterday and I have sense enough to know that you're not puttin' yourself out like this without wantin' some kind of pay back." She said in an attempt to provoke him.

"I wasn't born yesterday either and I know that there's a spirit behind that comment and I'll just consider the source." He calmly answered her. "Is there anything else you need to know?"

At that she narrowed her eyes and promptly and forcefully spit in his face.

"No you didn't just do that." Janice said then after deciding to come back in the room. "No you didn't!" She said again as she came towards her.

"Janice don't honey, c'mere." James told her after quickly intercepting her and leading her back out.

"Tell Sheila to get me out of here, I'm done with this." Kathryn said then. "I am done with this crap."

"It was easier for me to not react because I knew that that wasn't her." Douglas remarked half an hour later at the kitchen table with Janice, Chris and James.

"But we saw her do it, how do you mean it wasn't her?" Janice asked him. "And James if you hadn't stopped me, I might've hurt her." She said.

"That would've made the whole thing worse and you would've been sorry later on." Chris told her.

"Maybe not, she deserved to be hurt because you didn't say anything bad enough for her to do that." She insisted. "That was gross and I still don't understand how you just sat there and let her get by with that."

"Believe me when I tell you, it wasn't anything but the Holy Ghost that kept me from layin' her out." He began. "And that's not the worse thing that has ever happened to me but the difference is, I didn't have what it took to keep Junkyard under control." "It didn't matter if it was a woman, a kid, none of that; if you crossed me, you were in trouble which was why not too many people went there with me." He added, shaking his head.

"Do you remember that day when the dog that lived a couple of doors down from us walked up next to your car and laid his burdens down right next to your rims?' Chris asked him, starting to laugh.

"He never took another breath, I had to take him out." Douglas said, laughing with her. "And it was like he did it on purpose because a couple of days before that, I hit him with a rock because he was growlin' at Irene just because we were walkin' down the street and probably got too close to his yard."

"Didn't you hit him with a crowbar or somethin'?" Chris asked.

"That's what it was and I let him finish his business and walked up behind him and let him have it." "I don't think he ever knew what hit him."

"Where did Sheila go with her?" Janice suddenly asked.

"She's stayin' with mother, why?" Chris asked.

"I don't know, I was just wonderin'." She said, shrugging a little.

"Do you need to talk to her again?" James asked her.

"Not right now because I'm too upset and I might say somethin' really off because I just can't forget what I saw in there."

"Janice I really don't want you to let that keep you up at night because you know what?" Douglas asked her after a moment.

"What?" She asked as she wiped tears from her face.

"You'll make yourself miserable worryin' about what she might do, or what she's already done and you don't need that extra stress." He told her. "And the Lord sees everything that's goin on here and He knows how to take care of things like this."

She nodded a little. "I just feel like I'm causin' a lot of problems for everybody and I'm sorry."

"What do you think you're doin' that's causin' problems?" Chris asked her. "Is there anything else that you need from us or is there somethin' that we're not doin' to make you feel like that?"

She shook her head. "I feel like I owe everybody so much but right now, it's just me-

"Are you feelin' like that because of what she said in there a minute ago?" Douglas asked her.

"Why did she have to say that to you?" She asked him. "Everybody's mind is not in the gutter."

"I missed that one, what did she say?" Chris asked, surprised.

"She said that he was expectin' some kind of payback because of the way things have happened." James spoke up.

"Then when she didn't like my answer to that, that's when the drama started." He said humorously. "I'm over it Janice so do me a favor, don't think any more about it, and what we need to do is put this behind us and move on.".

CHAPTER 6

MARCH 23, MONDAY

"When Chris told me that you were gettin' ready to move out to the country Randy came up with this idea that we should save you the trouble of tryin' to sell this one." Donna said Monday night around six-thirty as she sat down at the table with James.

"Are you serious?" He asked as he opened a can of pop. "How come he didn't come with you?"

"He's home with the boys and I needed some air so here I am."

"Is Chris upstairs?"

"Yeah her and Janice are up there with the kids."

"Mother told me what happened in here Saturday, is she okay?"

"Yeah she is, she started workin' today and that's takin' her mind off of stuff."

"So she's ridin' with you every mornin'?"

"It works out that way." He said as the phone rang. "Speak to me Sheila Scott." He said, reading the caller i.d.

"James we just had an accident down here on forty-sixth street-

"Hold on, hold on Sheila, who's we?" "Who's with you?" He asked, hearing the panic in her voice.

"Me and Aunt Kathryn, we were almost there and somebody slid through the light up here and hit us on her side." She managed to say before quietly calling on the name of Jesus.

"Right up here on forty-sixth and Illinois?" He asked as he got up.

"Yeah, we were almost there." She said again as she tried to process what had just happened.

"Give me two minutes, I'm on my way."

"What happened James, you're scarin' me." Donna asked him.

"Sheila and Kathryn were on their way here and somebody slid into 'em, right down the street." "And I hear sirens, it must be bad." He said, starting out the door.

"I can't believe this James, tell me that this is not happenin.'" Sheila said a few minutes later as she sat in the front seat of the van as they waited on the police.

"Was she able to say anything after it happened?"

"She was just yellin' and cryin' and then she just sort of passed out." She said, still shaken up. "We were on the way to the airport and she asked me if we could stop at your house so she could see Janice before she went back home." She recalled. "And I started to tell her that we didn't really have time because her flight was at seven-fifteen."

"Hold on, this is Douglas." James said as his phone lit up.

"Tell me it's not bad." He said after he answered.

"Sheila's pretty much okay, we don't know yet about Kathryn but she said she was unconscious when they put her on the stretcher." James told him. "And as soon as she gets done talkin' to the police, I'm gonna go get Janice and we're headed to the hospital."

"I'm gonna stop to get mother and we'll meet you there."

"Were you the driver hon?" A nurse asked Sheila half an hour later outside the trauma unit.

She nodded a little. "I'm okay, I don't think I need to be checked out, I'm okay." She insisted as she kept her arm around Janice.

"Are you Mrs. Scott's daughter?" She asked Janice as she sat down on the other side of her.

"Yeah I am." She answered shortly.

"We'll have a trauma surgeon come out and talk to you in a few minutes but right now, we need to know if there is any other next of kin or a minister here that we can talk to?"

"Not right now but there's somebody that's on the way." Sheila said cautiously, fearing what she would say next.

"I have seen a lot of people come in after an accident but this is going to take a miracle and I really can't say much more than that but you should be prepared for the worst." She said in a matter of fact way. "We have a chaplain on staff here but if you prefer to have your own pastor or minister come in, that's entirely your decision." She continued as Sheila noticed Douglas and Frances get off the elevator.

"Am I gonna get to see her?" Janice asked then.

"Right now, we're trying to get her stabilized before she goes into surgery because she has a lot of internal injuries and I really wouldn't want you to see her just yet." She said as Sheila motioned Douglas to the other side of the waiting area while Frances sat down next to Janice.

"What are they sayin'?" He asked as they sat down.

"They're sayin' that it's gonna take a miracle for her to come out of this." She said, barely able to speak. "This is not real Douglas and if I had just told her that we didn't have time to stop at James and Chris' house, this wouldn't have happened." She said in regretful hindsight. "We were almost there and the other car lost control on some ice and just slid into us." She added as she got tissue from a nearby box.

"Was she goin' over there to talk to Janice before she left?" Douglas asked her.

"I guess so and if she had told me earlier that that's what she wanted to do, we could've left earlier but she just said all of a sudden, I need to go see Janice, can we stop." Sheila said, remembering the conversation.

"Did you get a chance to tell her that?' He asked, attempting to get an understanding.

She nodded. "She knows and it's like she's in a daze or somethin.'" "This whole thing has just blown her mind and she's sort of shut down, you know what I mean?"

"I know what you mean but she's gonna be alright." He said, assuring her. "Where did James go?"

"He went down to the place where they tow all the wrecks to get stuff out of my car." She said wearily.

"The impound yard downtown?"

"Yeah I guess you would know huh?" She said, keeping it together.

"As soon as you're up to it, you need to call the other insurance company and let them know what happened so they can get you a rental car and all of that." He instructed her. "Do you have the information from the driver that hit you?"

She nodded as she went into her purse. "The police got all of that and I'll do it when we get back." She said as she noticed the trauma physician come out and approach Janice and Frances.

"Here we go Douglas, brace yourself." She said as they got up and started towards them.

"You're all family here I'm guessing." The doctor spoke a moment later. "I'm Dr. Marshall and we just did an assessment of your mother's injuries and if she makes it through tonight, it will definitely be a miracle." He began. "She has a couple of broken ribs, one of her lungs has collapsed and right now, she's barely conscious which may indicate some kind of brain injury but we won't know that until we get a scan." He continued frankly. "We can allow two of you to go in but I wouldn't expect her to know or recognize anybody at this point and I'm putting it that way to prepare you for the worst." "She's been moved into the I.C.U. and we have her hooked up to monitors so don't be alarmed by all of that, it's normal procedure."

Then without hesitation, Douglas motioned for Janice to walk into the intensive care unit with him and as they approached Kathryn, she nearly doubled over at the sight of her. After he helped her into a nearby chair, he proceeded to her bedside and began to quietly but effectively petition the throne of God for complete and thorough healing of her injuries, knowing that there is nothing too hard for Him to do.

As the presence of the Lord began to fill the room, Janice for the first time experienced the peace and reality of the name of Jesus as he continued to allow the Holy Ghost to help him overcome any animosity towards her. It was a total release of faith coupled with a freedom to thank God for answering in His own time and manner.

"I really don't see how this can get any worse but I need to let you know how the conversation went when I called Roy to let him know about this accident." Frances told Douglas as they sat out in his car after Sheila went in the house an hour later. "And I know that you need to get back home so I'm not gonna keep you."

"Let me have it because you won't rest until you do."

"You're exactly right but he just came out and said that he would be here for Kathryn in a couple of days but Janice doesn't even need to know that he's comin.'" Frances said as she quoted her brother's words.

"Run that by me again?" He said after a moment.

"You heard me right and it took everything in me not to hang up in his ear but the Lord said otherwise."

"So how does he think he's gonna come and go without seein' her?" He asked. "This is craziness."

"I thought you might think that but this doesn't surprise me Douglas." There is somethin' missing there and now isn't the time to try to figure all of this out but I just thought I'd run that by you."

"Have you talked to Marie yet?"

"She'll be here by the end of this week she said, she can't get off work 'til then but I'm tellin' you honey, this is just the beginning so you just keep lettin' God help you and it'll all work out." She added as his phone went off.

"Yeah Chris, what's up?" He asked.

"You're not home yet are you?" She asked him.

"Not quite, your mother is busy workin' me over right now."

"Can you stop back by here when you leave there?" "I know that you just brought Janice back but she said that she needs to talk to you."

"I can be there in fifteen minutes."

"And I called Irene so she won't be worried about you."

"I'm on my way."

"That was quick, you meant that didn't you?' Chris asked him as he came in the back door.

"You sounded serious."

"I asked her if it was anything that me or James could do so we wouldn't have to bother you again."

"You're not botherin' me." "Where is she?"

"She's in the livin' room waitin' on you." "I'll be upstairs."

"How come you're sittin' in the dark hon?" He asked her a minute later as he came in and turned on a lamp.

"I think better in the dark." She said quietly.

"What're you thinkin' about?" He asked her as he sat down in a nearby chair. "Are you worried about your mother?"

"I didn't get a chance to thank you for doin' that at the hospital." She began. "And it was like I felt somethin' in there when you were prayin' for her and it was sort of scary."

"What you felt was the power of God in there and that's not anything to be afraid of." He told her. "That's a good thing and that's the reason we'll see the miracle that they were talkin' about." He added with confidence. "It looks pretty bad now but the worse it looks now, the more glory the Lord will get for doin' this for her."

"But how did you do that after what she did to you in here the other night?"

"I was able to do that because that's what the Lord led me to do and I don't have any choice but to forgive her for that and move on." He said after a moment. "I had to look past what I saw on the surface and love her soul like God does."

She nodded a little.

"Does that make sense to you?"

"I want the Holy Ghost Douglas."

"That's a good thing too but I wasn't expectin' to hear you say it like this." He responded after a moment. "How long have you been feelin' like that?"

"I mean I can't do this by myself and after tonight, it was like I couldn't believe what I was seein'." She managed to say. "Things are just so much different here and it's probably because just about everybody has the Holy Ghost". She said in frustration.

"You're soundin' like you're on the defensive about it." He said. "And if you're feelin' like the Lord is dealin' with you, it's for you and not just because of somebody else." "It's for your salvation, it's your power, your strength and anything else that you allow it to be for you and after so long, somebody else will see your life and want it because of what they see in you."

"And I guess that's what's goin' on huh?"

"You're the only one that can answer that but it's good that you're lettin' the Lord talk to you and it doesn't matter what you might've heard about this, it's real and it's a promise that the Lord made to anybody that wants it." He finished as he began to feel the anointing of the spirit around them. "Have you been able to get to church at all since you've been here?"

"I went one Sunday night with Ruth and Sheila and that was right after I got here." She said wearily. "I just haven't gone back."

"If you ever feel like you need to go back, don't let anything stop you." "And I'll tell you somethin' about the Holy Ghost and if you don't remember anything else I've said tonight, just know that it can fall on you whenever, or wherever your heart gets to the place where God wants it." "Don't be afraid of it because it'll be the best thing that ever happens to you."

"Wow."

"Your Aunt Frances told me about a girl that was in her eighth grade class, probably about sixty years ago." "They were in class standin' up and sayin' the Lord's prayer in the mornin' like they used to do and then out of nowhere she started speakin' in this language that she had never spoken before and they thought she was crazy but the Holy Ghost fell on that girl right there on the spot."

"But where does God want your heart to be?" "And I'm sorry if I don't understand all of this but it is what it is." She said apologetically.

"Janice do you know how glad I am to be havin' this conversation with you?" Douglas asked her then. "Somebody had to sit down with me and my no good Junkyard self and lay it out to help me understand that there was nothin' more important and precious than my soul." "People are leavin' out of here without God every day and it's time to run for your life because nobody knows how long they have, and when I saw that mess out on the street that night, it rocked my world as hard as I thought I was."

She nodded a little and didn't speak as she continued to intently listen to him.

"And when the Lord sees that you're ready to leave all of this stuff that the devil gets you involved in and that you're turnin' away from it, He sees repentance." "Then that's when the Holy Ghost comes in to you and changes the way you act and think and it's the power to overcome yourself because you can't do it on your own." He continued. "And I'm not makin' any of this up, it's all in the scripture and if you feel like you need to talk about this to any of us, wake us up, keep us up if you have to because this is your soul honey." "We love you and we have to do whatever it takes to help you get through all of this." He said as he got up to leave as she slowly stood up. "And just like you let me know that you want the Holy Ghost, you tell the Lord the same thing because He's the only one that can give it to you and He can't go back on His promise."

"Thanks again for comin' back and I'll try not to worry about mother because I know that everybody's prayin' for her.".

MARCH 24, TUESDAY

"She won't know that you're here because we have her sedated but if you would like to go in and sit for a few minutes, that's fine." An I.C.U. nurse spoke to Janice and Sheila Tuesday evening at the hospital. "And actually she's doing better than we expected her to be so we may be able to move her in a day or two."

"You haven't seen her yet have you?" Janice asked as they walked towards her area.

She shook her head. "But I still remember how she was right after we got hit so I know this is a God thing that she's still here."

"I almost passed out when I came in here with Douglas and saw her for the first time." "She didn't even look like herself." She added as they cautiously approached her bedside a minute later.

"I'll be right back Janice, hold up." Sheila said then, going back out as her phone vibrated.

"Is Janice with you?" Irene asked her a moment later.

"We're at the hospital, why?"

"How's Aunt Kathryn?" She asked after a moment.

"She's still out because they have her sedated but she's better than they thought she'd be." She answered. "And you don't sound right, please don't give me any more bad news."

"Marie just called mother and told her that uncle Roy died in his sleep overnight." "She was pickin' him up around two-thirty to take him to the airport and he wouldn't come to the door so she used her key to get in the house and found him still in the bed from last night." Irene explained. "This doesn't seem real but go ahead and tell Janice, and Douglas is gonna meet both of you at mother's house." She said slowly and deliberately. "He's pickin' Chris up because James doesn't want her out by herself later on tonight and I'll call you later over there."

"Had you talked to him at all since you got here honey?" Frances asked Janice an hour later in her living room with Chris, Douglas, and Sheila.

She shook her head. "The last thing I said to him was that I was gettin' out of his way and that was right after I told 'em I was pregnant." She said as she struggled to keep her composure.

"So it was him that told you that you needed to leave and not so much your mother?" Douglas asked her.

"It was her too but she didn't wanna cross him so she just went along with it." Frances spoke up. "And I know that this is a lot to deal with at one time but this is why we're here." She added.

"Is Marie still comin' or is she stayin' there to take care of stuff in D.C.?" Chris asked.

"That's another thing, she wants you to be there for his funeral Janice and I almost told her that you're not up to it but she needs to hear that from you." Frances told her.

"I really don't need to think about that, I've got too much other stuff goin' on." She insisted irritably.

"And she should realize that you're goin' through enough here and you don't need any extra stress." Chris spoke up as she started to become agitated. "Too much stuff like this can make you miscarry and she needs to remember that."

"At least Aunt Kathryn made it through the night." Sheila said then as she tried to interject something positive. "But maybe we don't need to go back up there 'til she wakes up."

"Then somebody has to let her know about Roy and that's not gonna be an easy thing." Frances said as Douglas noticed Janice cringe at that thought and at that, he got up and came towards her while simultaneously motioning Chris and Sheila over to the sofa where they were sitting.

"Time is out for talkin, we can't just sit here and watch this go on like this." He said, lowering his voice. Then as she felt the power of God through his touch on her shoulder, she began to yield herself as her lips began to stammer uncontrollably as the four of them began to intercede on her behalf for comfort and strength.

"Believe God, He's right here." Douglas said as his spirit began to bear witness with hers as her language instantly changed as evidence that the Holy Ghost had come as promised. As she began to realize what was happening she let herself go and freely allowed the Lord to have His way with her while the spirit of God clearly gave the utterance.

For the next half hour they rejoiced with her as the burdens of her heart seemed to roll away in comparison to the joy unspeakable that she was experiencing.

"I was just wonderin' if she knew about havin' to get baptized too." Sheila said as she and Douglas sat in the kitchen while Chris and Frances waited with Janice in the living room.

"I'm not sure but I really don't think that'll be a problem." He said as he started calling home to talk to Irene. "Watch this." He added as he put his phone on speaker.

"How's it goin' over there?" Irene asked a moment later.

"Are you sittin' down?"

"Why?" She asked with hesitation in her voice.

"Janice just got the Holy Ghost over here, you're missin' it." He said, purposely 'rubbing it in.'

"What??"

"You heard me right."

"I'll call you back."

"She lost it." Sheila said after she quickly hung up.

"I knew she would and this is how it's supposed to be, you shouldn't have to work for what the scripture calls a gift." He said with conviction.

"She told me that you had talked to her last night and evidently somethin' got through."

"There were a couple of things that she didn't quite understand and we were talkin about Kathryn then just all of a sudden, she told me that she wanted the Holy Ghost". He said reflecting back. "And that really took me by surprise because of how she said it."

"It was probably because of what she saw you do last night that really affected her." "She was expectin' you to be just the opposite of the way you were with Aunt Kathryn and that might've been all it took to help her out, you know what I'm sayin'?"

"But I'm tellin' you, my first instinct was to lay her out and it wasn't anything but the Lord that stopped me." He admitted to her.

"And that's my point, the Lord allowed her to see those two things and that probably has a lot to do with what's goin' on in there now." Sheila concluded. "I love it."

"So how do you feel after yesterday, did you get a chance to talk to the other insurance company?"

"I did and they're goin' out to the impound place tomorrow to look at it and probably total it but God's good anyhow even though I'm sort of sore right now." She said as Frances came in then with her arm around Janice, still overwhelmed by her second birth experience.

"Tell me what you have dear heart." Douglas told her a moment later as they embraced in a manner that communicated to her that the Lord had provided a spiritual as well as a much needed father figure in him.

"I have the Holy Ghost." She managed to say through joyful tears and before she could say anything further, she began to speak in tongues once again as she let him go and began to walk through the house, rejoicing in the God of her salvation.

"James is comin' to get us so you won't have to go out of your way Douglas." Chris told him an hour later, still at the kitchen table with he and Frances.

"I made her go lay down for awhile 'til he gets here, she's had a rough couple of days." Frances said, referring to Janice. "And Sheila clocked out too." She said as she poured Douglas a cup of coffee.

"So did you call Marie back?" Chris asked.

"I'll call her in the mornin' and let her know that I'll be there but Janice doesn't need to make that trip, she needs to be here when Kathryn wakes up." She said after a moment. "And if she has a problem with that, she'll just have to get over it."

"Do you think she'll be able to come back with you after the funeral?" Chris asked her.

"She needs to if she can because Janice doesn't need to deal with this by herself and I know that she has all of us, but she's her mother too."

"Will she be able to get off work for all of this?" Douglas asked Chris.

"I don't know why not unless there might be a problem because she just started but James would know, we'll find out."

"And you do know that you have another daughter now don't you?" Frances asked Douglas as she sat down next to Chris.

"I'm more than willin' to do that but that's pretty much up to her." He answered after a moment. "I'll make sure that she knows that I'm available but I want her to realize that I won't be all up in her business unless she needs help with somethin.'"

"Believe me Douglas, you have another daughter now." Chris told him as she emphasized what Frances had just spoken to him. "She's already adopted James as her brother so between the two of you, she's gonna be alright."

"Number one she has the Holy Ghost now so that's more than half the battle but like I said, I'm more than willin' to do what I can and I'll make sure she knows it." Douglas told her. "Does she have a bible?"

"I don't think so, I've never seen her with one."

"Do me a favor and go get her one and tell her that it's my birthday gift to her." He said as he handed her a twenty dollar bill from his wallet.

"Her birthday was last month." She said before realizing what he meant.

"Yeah but this one tonight is the one that really matters." He said as James came in the door.

"Don't rub it in, I already know." He said as he walked over to Frances and put his arm around her shoulder. "Are you okay?"

"I'm okay honey, I'm goin' out there tomorrow in Janice's place because she needs to be here for Kathryn." She said, filling him in.

"Where is she?"

"I made her go to bed for a minute because she's been through a lot the last couple of days and we don't need any more bad drama."

"Will it be a problem for her to be off work since she just started?" Douglas asked him as he sat down next to Chris.

"She can take off but they won't pay her for funeral leave 'til she has sixty days in."

"I can see her goin' to work anyway, this doesn't seem to really be botherin' her that much and I don't know whether that's a bad or a good thing." Chris commented.

"It might take a minute for it to sink in and if and when it does, she has her help.' Douglas remarked. "Mark my words"...

CHAPTER 7

MARCH 26, THURSDAY

"Now I know what you were talkin' about when you were tellin' us about how you felt when you got baptized." Janice remarked Thursday night on the hospital elevator with Irene and Douglas after taking Frances to the airport. "I felt like I was walkin' on air last night."

"And if you ever start to feel guilty or condemned about somethin' that went on before just remember that it's all under the blood of Jesus." Douglas told her.

"When I woke up yesterday mornin' I thought I had dreamed Tuesday night then I started feelin' stuff all over again." She said as they stepped off the elevator.

"It wouldn't be quite fair to keep something like this from her but it might cause a set back as far as her recovery goes." Kathryn's doctor remarked a few minutes later as he consulted with them.

"She's not still unconscious is she?" Irene asked.

"She's no longer sedated but we have her on a low dose of morphine for pain control." "It's only been seventy-two hours so she still has a long road ahead of her and as her minister, I know that you're thanking the man upstairs that she's pulling through."

"We know that it's God healin' her but I'm not her minister." Douglas said, quickly correcting him. "Did somebody tell you that?" He asked out of curiosity.

"We were going by what happened the night of her accident but whatever the case, she's still here because of someone's prayers, we can assure you of that." He replied. "Are you her daughter?" He asked Janice.

She nodded. "Is it okay for two of us to go in there because I don't really feel comfortable doin' this by myself."

"I can allow two at a time and depending on how she reacts to you should determine how long you stay." "And if you feel comfortable about letting her know about your dad, be really cautious about how you speak because we don't want any setbacks."

"C'mon Janice, I'll go in here with you." Irene told her as she stood up. "You can do this."

As they walked into the room, Kathryn slowly turned her head towards them as she slowly opened her eyes. Then without speaking, she held out her left hand while tears began to flow freely down her face.

"What took you so long to come?" She asked slowly and deliberately as she started to bask in self-pity.

"We were here right after the accident but you were unconscious mom." Janice told her as she leaned over her with a tissue to wipe her tears.

"How long have I been here, what day is this?" She asked, disoriented and confused.

"The accident happened on Monday and this is Thursday." Irene told her.

"I'm tryin' to remember what happened." She said, holding her head.

"If you can't remember that's okay for right now, we just want you to get some rest so you can get better." Janice told her. "Are you hurtin' anywhere?"

Instead of answering her question, she suddenly began to recall being in the car with Sheila and let out a moan as she recoiled in mental anguish. At that point, Irene motioned Janice aside to talk out of earshot of her.

"Do you think she's ready to hear about Uncle Roy?"

"I don't think she's quite strong enough but I can't keep puttin' it off because she's gonna start askin' me where he is and then I have to tell her."

"Stay with her, I'm gettin' Douglas in here." She said as she turned to leave the room.

"Is Sheila okay?" She finally asked Janice a minute later as she sat on the side of her bed.

"She didn't get hurt and she's been up here to see you but they had you sedated and I don't think you knew she was here." She told her as she noticed Douglas come in for her support, much to her relief.

"But why isn't your father here, he's had time to get here." She asked her, perplexed by his absence.

At that, she turned to him for direction after he had purposely stood back from them and allowed her to exercise her God given power and strength, as he nodded for her to give her an answer.

"He was supposed to be here Tuesday night but Marie called and told us that he died in his sleep before he could get here." She managed to say as she finally gave in to her grief and sorrow for their loss, despite the strained relationship that she had had with him. At that moment as Douglas noticed that she was too overcome to continue, he came over to the bedside and gently escorted her out into the hallway where Irene took over before he went back into the room to talk to Kathryn.

For the next few minutes, after he pulled a nearby chair from a corner to her bedside, neither spoke a word as she kept her face covered with both hands, quietly sobbing while shaking her head in pain and shock.

"Is there anything you need for us to do for you Kathryn?" He finally spoke.

She couldn't answer and as she suddenly recognized his voice, she became even more remorseful and unable to speak. Then as Janice came back in after composing herself, Douglas got up and stepped back out of her way as she sat down on the bed, ready to do whatever it took to console her.

"We'll be right outside the door if you need us." Douglas told her as he lowered his voice and left the room to give them their privacy.

She nodded and thanked him as she got a couple of tissues from a nearby dispenser to dry Kathryn's face once again.

"Why is all of this happenin' to me?" "Roy wouldn't leave me like this." She finally said.

"Nobody has the answers to any of that so all we can do is deal with it and let God help us." She spoke before she knew what would come out.

"I can't deal with this right now, I need to be put back to sleep before I can think about this anymore." She said after a moment.

"Are you sure?" Janice asked her. "If you want me to, I can call a nurse in here and she can give you a pill."

She nodded a little and started to languish in more self-pity and disbelief.

"We love you and we're prayin' for you." Janice told her then after kissing her on one of her cheeks. "I'll let one of the nurses know that you need somethin' to make you sleep."

"This is all that we have to sign, we don't have to go through a realtor or anything?" Donna asked at the kitchen table with Randy, James and Chris.

"I'm your realtor slash seller and this is your purchase agreement ma'am." James said as he began signing his and Chris' copy. "But there's no commission."

I'm takin' a picture of this, look up and say cheese everybody." 'Nita said then pointing her phone towards them. "Are you gonna cry James?"

"I'll still be able to come in and out of here sometimes so it's not like the man on the street is buyin' it, it's still in the family."

"So your new house is gonna be basically the same floorplan as this one is?" Randy asked him.

"We're puttin' a family room to the right of the entryway and the rest of it is pretty much the same except the rooms might be a little bigger." James said. "I'm still workin' on the print but they're breakin' ground on it next week."

"So we can move in here sometime in May?" Donna asked him. "Please don't say three months because I don't wanna be movin' and havin' this baby at the same time."

"When is your due date?"

"June fifteenth so this is gonna be close, I'm gettin' worried just thinkin' about that."

"Quit bein' so dramatic, it's all under control." 'Nita told her. "What do you think is gonna happen?"

"I've heard of movin' makin' you go into labor and I don't need any drama like that." She said as Irene, Douglas and Janice came in the back door.

"This looks serious." Douglas said, noticing the paperwork spread out on the table.

"We just bought this house, it's official." Donna told him. "And I haven't seen you since your awesome news." She told Janice as she took her jacket off. "How do you feel?"

"Awesome." She said immediately. "And I know that I'm supposed to be messed up right now but I got it out tonight and God is helpin' me to move on." She said with strength in her voice.

"Don't you love it?" Douglas asked as he sat down.

"I really do 'cause we've really been prayin' for you and I like to know that God answers prayer." She said as she folded up their documents into an envelope.

"They're too quiet up there, are they all sleep?" Irene asked.

"Some of 'em are and they know that I don't play, when I say sit down and watch the video, that's what cousin 'Nita means." She said as she started to run dishwater.

"What are they watchin'?" James asked her.

"They're watchin' Dennis the Menace and they won't get tired of it" "They like the part on the railroad tracks where he ties up the hobo."

"So how did it go?" Chris asked then. "Did you tell her what was goin' on?"

"I did and it was hard for her but I had to tell her why he wasn't here." Janice said after a moment. "And I lost it too but I feel better that I did." She admitted.

"I had to leave, it was too much for me to watch so I made Douglas go in there." Irene said. "But you did good, she'll be okay after all of this settles down."

"Is Marie comin' back with mother after the funeral?"

"They'll be here Sunday afternoon around two and Janice don't let her make you feel bad for not goin', you probably did the right thing by stayin' here for your mother." Chris told her. "Sometimes you just have to do what you have to do.".

MARCH 29, SUNDAY

"We're stayin' with Aunt Frances but I had James bring us over here so we could go to the hospital together." Marie remarked Sunday afternoon with Chris as they sat in the living room. "And I'm really havin' a hard time wrappin' my head around all of this, it's been crazy." She added with bewilderment in her voice.

"What has mother told you?"

"She has told me so much stuff that I can't really process it which is why I need to talk to you because this is where Janice is stayin.'"

"It's not really a big deal how it happened." Chris began. "She just called here one Sunday night and said that she needed somebody to come and pick her up at the airport, and what we didn't know was that she had told 'Nita that she was comin' and we couldn't just leave her out there."

"Wait a second, she just showed up here without tellin' anybody that she was comin?"

She nodded. "And when she got here, I made her call Aunt Kathryn to let her know where she was so they wouldn't be worried about her but I think she just left her a voicemail without actually talkin' to her." Chris recalled.

"So from what Aunt Frances told me, she left because they told her that she couldn't stay home because she would be an embarrassment to them at church." Marie said.

"That's pretty much the understandin' that we got about it and we didn't know that she was pregnant 'til about three weeks ago." Chris told her.

"What did she do, just all of a sudden say one day, oh by the way, I'm pregnant?" Marie said, becoming irritated.

"Douglas was the first one that she told and he just happened to be at the right time and place because she couldn't keep it anymore."

"And that's what I'm tryin' to figure out." "When Aunt Frances told me that, I'm like, really?" "The only thing I know about him is that he's Irene's husband and he used to work with Jerry a thousand years ago but I've never met him so I don't understand that either."

"She was afraid to tell me and James because she didn't want the same thing to happen all over again." Chris explained. "And Marie, we don't need any more drama in here which is why I would rather tell you what's goin' on before you jump on her with it."

"But you can believe I'm gonna talk to her and let her know that none of this would've happened if she had just kept herself at home where she belonged." "She could've stayed with me and Jerry if she had just called and told me what was goin' on instead of flyin' across country like this and trippin' everybody else out with her problems." She said as she continued to angrily vent.

"Is there any else you need to say Marie?" Chris asked her calmly. "Because like I said, I'd rather take it from you than have her have to deal with this all over again."

"Where is she anyway?" James said somethin' about her stayin' after church for some kind of young people's meetin' but I thought she'd be here by now." She said as she attempted to calm herself.

"Did you try to call her and let her know that you're here?"

"I haven't yet but I'm just frustrated by the whole thing Chris." She said as she began to think about Kathryn. "Mother wouldn't be layin' up in the hospital half dead if she hadn't done this and I'm just havin' a hard time with this whole crazy thing."

"But it's all under control now though Marie." She's gonna be okay but it's just gonna take awhile and it could've gone the other way if we hadn't gotten busy and prayed her through that first night."

"Was it that bad?"

"They weren't expectin' her to make it and they were tellin' us to get the family together and to have the chaplain come and all of that but the Lord has all of this under control honey." Chris told her. "Janice is gettin' herself together and that's because she has seen things happen around here that've let her know that God is real."

"What else has gone on that I don't know about?"

"For one thing, she got the Holy Ghost Tuesday night and that's the only reason that she's been able to deal with all of this without fallin' apart." She said as the phone rang.

"Hey Chris, is Marie there yet?' Irene asked her.

"Yeah I'm sittin' here talkin' to her now."

"Tell her that Janice is on her way, Douglas is bringin' her and 'Nita home so they'll be there in a few minutes."

"You look so different honey, come in here and talk to me." Marie told Janice fifteen minutes later after she and 'Nita came in the front door.

"I feel different, I feel a lot different than I did the last time I talked to you." She said as they sat down on the sofa together.

"Where's what's his name, Douglas?"

"He let us out at the front, he's back in the kitchen with James and Chris." Janice answered cautiously. "Did you need to talk to him too?"

"Maybe later but it's you I'm tryin' to figure out." "And how is mother, when did you see her last?"

"We went out there last night and she's a little better than she was Thursday when I told her about daddy dyin'."

"Do you have any idea how many people asked me where you were at his funeral?"

"I couldn't be in both places and I just figured that I'd be better off here with mother, she's the one that's still here, he's gone."

"So you don't feel anything about him at all?"

"It's not so much that, but you weren't there when I first told them about this Marie." She began. "It was like, get out of my sight, you don't need to be around here embarrassin' us and this and that so that was when I got out of there as soon as I could get a plane ticket." "They made me feel like dirt."

"Why didn't you call me Janice, you could've come and stayed with me and Jerry." Marie said, becoming more agitated.

"I thought about that but at the time, all I wanted to do was get as far away from there as I could and that's when I called 'Nita and told her that I would be here that Sunday night."

"And nobody knew that you were pregnant?" Marie asked in an attempt to condemn her.

She shook her head and immediately remembered what Douglas had told her how her past had been cleaned up by the blood of Jesus the moment of her water baptism in His name.

"So how long did you think you were gonna be able to keep it Janice, you're already startin' to get a bump." Marie continued in her efforts to bring her down.

"I knew that I had to come out with it and one night when I was babysittin' at Douglas and Irene's house, we were talkin' and I don't even remember exactly about what but he could tell that I was holdin' somethin' back and I just spit it out." "I sat there and cried and I looked up and he was too."

"You're kiddin." Marie said.

Janice shook her head a little. "And I know that he was our father and all of that but he never took the time to sit down and listen to any problems that I was havin' or any of that and that's probably why I got hooked up so easy with Craig."

"Does he know?"

"I sent him a text right after I took a pregnancy test and he called me back and said that this was my problem and to leave him out of it." Janice said, remembering the conversation. "He hung up on me and that was it." She added, shrugging a little.

"And you're just gonna let him get by without payin' support or anything Janice?" "How do you think you'll be able to take care of yourself and this baby too?"

"I'm takin' this a little at a time Marie." She said as she refused to get caught in her trap. "I've got another chance to get stuff done right and I'm not about to go back to where I was because I wasn't gettin' anywhere."

"So there's no way that you're comin' back home?"

She shook her head. "I'm done with D.C. because too many negative things happened to me there and I'm startin' over here." She emphasized. "Did Jerry come with you?" She asked, changing the subject.

"He rented a car at the airport and he went to see his mother." "But he said he'd be over here later, he wanted to maybe run into Douglas before he goes back."

"How long are you gonna be here?"

"That depends how quick mother can travel but if she's as bad off as Aunt Frances said she was, it might be awhile but they gave me a six week leave of absence so I don't have to worry about leavin' her here." Marie said. "And if she hadn't been here in the first place, we wouldn't be goin' through all of this." She persisted.

"But I told her on the phone that I wasn't comin' back but she came anyway Marie." Janice came back. "And I'm really sorry that this happened to her but if she hadn't come like she did, I wouldn't have seen some things that helped me to know that everybody's not a hypocrite."

"But you're gonna find hypocrites wherever you are, I don't care if they go to church with you or work with you or if it's family or whatever so you don't have to go there with me Janice, I know better than that."

"But I know what I saw in here that tripped me out and I don't know what you've seen or haven't seen but the day she got here, she was in here talkin' to Douglas about all of this and then for no reason, she sat in that chair over there and spit in his face." Janice recalled. "And God is helpin' me to forgive her for that but it's somethin' that I won't be able to forget for a long time."

"When did this happen?' Marie asked, shocked.

"It was a week ago yesterday and all he did was clean it off with a handkerchief and kept it movin.'" "She got up and walked out like it wasn't a big deal and then two days later, he's at the hospital prayin' over her like she was his mother and that's probably why she made it through that first night."

"Was she awake for all of that?"

"They had her put out so I don't think she knows about that but when I saw him do that after what she did, it was like all of this stuff about the Lord that I had heard everybody talk about was really true." Janice said. "And all of that might not sound like a really big deal to you but that's what made me know that I needed some big time help."

"That's pretty unreal." Marie said after a moment. "Is there a bathroom down here?" She asked her as she stood up and looked around.

"Right there in the hallway." Janice said, feeling a sense of relief that their conversation had temporarily ended.

"I told you that you would survive." Douglas told her a minute later as she sat down at the kitchen table with him, James and Chris.

"Where is she, is everything okay?" Chris asked her as she opened a jar of baby food for Byron in the high chair.

"Yeah we had a few words but it's all good." Janice began. "I just had to explain a couple of things and it is what it is."

"Does she want to go to the hospital tonight or wait 'til tomorrow mornin'?" James asked her.

"If Jerry gets here in time we might go tonight but I think tomorrow would be better so we can stay longer." Janice said after a moment. "Visitin' hours are over at eight."

"Mommy that lady in there is bleedin' really bad." Patti announced then as she came into the kitchen.

At that, James and Douglas quickly got up from the table and followed her towards the half bathroom in the hallway and discovered Marie standing over the sink bleeding from one of her wrists.

"Go back in there with your mom." James told her as he closed the door to shield her from seeing any more. "Tell her I said to call nine one one."

"Honey what are you doin'?" Douglas quietly asked her as he stood behind her while grabbing a hand towel from one of the bars and wrapping it around her self-inflicted wound to stop any further bleeding.

She didn't answer but began moaning from the pain as they attempted to keep her from passing out by lying her down on the floor until E.M.T. help arrived.

"Is this really happenin'?" Janice asked as she and Douglas stood outside the bathroom door ten minutes later while Marie was being treated by emergency personnel.

"It's happenin' but this is one of those things that you have to give to God because it's too big for us to figure out." He told her. "I'll try to talk to her if she'll let me but this is somethin' that's probably been in her mind before today and this was her way of lettin' us know that she needs help."

"So you don't think she wanted to go out like that?"

"If she had really wanted to, she would have waited 'til she was by herself." He told her. "People that kill themselves don't do it when somebody else is around."

"And if Patti hadn't come down here and seen her in there, it might've worked." Janice said, shaking her head a little.

"That was ordered by God and nobody can tell me otherwise." Douglas said, before he motioned her into the living room.

"Did I do somethin' wrong?" Janice asked him cautiously as she sat down.

"Did she say anything to you earlier that might have somethin' to do with this?" "And you didn't do anything wrong, relax."

"We were just talkin' about mother and then she went off into all this other stuff about my problems." She answered after thinking a moment. "And your name came up but I can't think of anything that we talked about that would make her want to kill herself."

"You don't happen to have Jerry's number do you?" "He needs to be here."

"I can probably find it on her phone." She said as she noticed Marie's purse on the floor next to the sofa where she had been sitting.

"Hold on a second before you do that." He said as he heard the bathroom door open. "And just pray." He told her as he walked out to meet one of the technicians.

"We have her stabilized and stitched up and we gave her something for her pain." She began. "Are you a family member sir?"

"Her sister is here if you need a signature for this." He said as Janice overheard and came towards them.

"She had a pretty close call, she's lucky and whenever we come across a suicide attempt like this, we have to refer the person to one of these agencies so you'll be getting a call in the next couple of days." She said as she handed Janice a list of help line telephone numbers.

"She doesn't live here, does that make any difference?" Janice asked her.

"That's something that you will have to discuss with the agency that calls but I wouldn't waste any time getting her some help because more often than not, if it doesn't work the first time, there will be another try and you don't want that."

"He's got his phone off, it goes right to his voicemail." Janice remarked back in the kitchen an hour later after trying Jerry's number several times.

"Did you leave him a message or text him?" Chris asked her.

"I've done both and it's like he's ignorin' me on purpose." She said as she checked Marie's phone again. "Is Patti okay?"

"Yeah we talked to her and I don't think she knows what's goin' on but if she hadn't come in here and let us know what she saw, there's no tellin' what would've happened." She said as she started the coffee maker on the counter. "And I have a feelin' that this is gonna be a long night; Douglas has already called Irene to let her know that it'll be a minute before he gets home."

"Is he in there with her?"

"Not yet, she's still sleep in the livin' room and they gave her a sedative so she might be out for awhile but James took Douglas out to the lot, I think they needed some air."

"I've seen how tight they are and I think that's really a good thing."

"It is 'cause James doesn't have any brothers and three sisters so he comes in handy, no kiddin.'" Chris said. "But Douglas tried to leave earlier and he said he just couldn't before he gets a chance to talk to Marie so like I said, it's gonna be a long night."

"So this is why Janice has been blowin' up my phone for the last couple of hours?" Jerry asked an hour later with Douglas as they sat at the dining room table, where they could watch Marie still asleep on the sofa in the living room through the closed French doors which separated the rooms.

"One of Chris' kids came downstairs and went in the bathroom and saw her in there bleedin' over the sink." Douglas told him. "She had just been in there talkin' to Janice and I asked her if she remembered anything that she might've said that was unusual or whatever but she couldn't come up with anything."

"Man I appreciate you hangin' around for us like this but I'm just as much in the dark as you are and we have problems that we need to work out like everybody else but this is out of nowhere."

"Things like this usually are but I'm stickin' around because of what I saw in there." Douglas said. "She was serious and the only reason I think that she wants help is because she did it when we were around to see just how desperate she is." He added with genuine concern for her.

"She told me that she's never met you, so you're tellin' me that today's the first time you've laid eyes on her and you're takin' up your time like this for her?" Jerry asked him in skeptical astonishment. "Man if I didn't know you from a few years back, I wouldn't trust you no farther than I could throw you."

"And I wouldn't blame you a bit because when I put myself in your place, I totally see where you're comin' from but you do know me from a few years back so you answered your own issue." Douglas told him as he attempted to keep it light while at the same time focusing on the severity of the situation. "I've been where she is so I know what it feels like and that might be why I couldn't leave a couple of hours ago like I tried to."

"You are kiddin' me man."

"Can't kid about things like that and if I didn't have a prayin' mother-in-law, I might not be sittin' here talkin' to you so there's no reason for me to cut out when I see somebody else goin' through the same thing that I did."

"That is some deep stuff, I had no idea." Jerry said, shocked. "You don't mind if I ask you what was goin' on do you?"

"Long story short, I saw the head of a friend of mine come off right in front of me in a motorcycle accident and for a week, that's all I could see in my mind, over and over again." He answered, thinking back. "And it got to the point where I couldn't deal with it anymore and I came really close to takin' myself out with my forty-five."

"But you had a prayin' mother-in-law."

"And love her to death to this day and that was pretty close to fifteen years ago but the Lord won't allow me to forget how He spared me from goin' into eternity that night so who am I to ignore somethin' like this?"

"The man upstairs must've had a plan for you then to keep you alive after all of that." Jerry said as they noticed Marie slowly try to sit up and hold her head with her bandaged arm.

"Go see about your wife, I'll be in here somewhere if you feel like you might need some help."

"You wanna tell me what's goin' on with you Marie?" Jerry asked her five minutes later as he sat down after helping her to sit up after she lay back down.

"When did you get here?" She asked, confused and disoriented. "How long have I been sleep?"

"You don't remember what happened?" He asked her as he lifted her left arm for her to see the bandage.

"How come it didn't work?"

"Why in the world are you talkin' crazy, have I done somethin' to you to make you feel so out of it like this?" He impatiently persisted with her. "I'm really tryin' to find out what the problem is but if you don't open up, I can't help you." He continued as he began to raise his voice in aggravation.

"That's not soundin' good and maybe this is why you couldn't leave earlier." Chris told Douglas then after overhearing him.

"It's all yours man, I give up." Jerry said then as he came back into the kitchen and started out the back door. "I'll be out here." He said as he went outside to smoke a cigarette.

"I need you to come in here with me because we don't need any more stuff goin' down than what we've already had." Douglas told her as he slowly and deliberately got up from the table. "Where's James?"

"He's in there workin' on blueprints in the office and he told me that he needs to stay out of any more of this, he saw enough before."

"He told me the same thing but this is his house and he needs to know what's goin' on." "Is Janice still here?"

"I told her to go to bed because I could tell that this is workin' on her too, and it might not be such a bad idea for her to go stay with mother for a couple of days just to get away from all of this for a minute."

"Marie?" Douglas said as he and Chris walked into the living room where they found her sitting on the sofa with her head back and eyes closed as if in deep thought. "How do you feel?"

She didn't verbally answer but attempted to use body language by beating up on herself with her fists to convey to them her feelings of hopelessness and heartfelt guilt over an unspoken issue which Douglas began to understand with Holy Ghost given discernment. Then without speaking, Chris went over and tightly embraced her to prevent any further injuries while allowing her own compassionate tears to flow.

Then as Douglas began to allow his Spirit to speak within him, the revelation of Marie's incestuous incident with Roy caused him to sit down in a nearby chair and wait until she had calmed down enough to talk to him.

"When did it happen Marie?" He asked her a few minutes later in his effort to let her know that it had been revealed to him what had taken place and too, for his own confirmation of this Word of Knowledge.

"Are you Douglas?" She managed to ask him as she brought herself to look at him after suddenly remembering his voice from the bathroom.

"Yeah I am and I'm harmless so don't be afraid to talk to me." He answered her. "I've been where you are so I understand how this can eat you alive and make you want to do somethin' desperate like kill yourself but you would've been in far worse shape than you are now so just begin to thank God that He didn't allow that to happen." He continued. "And nobody is forcin' you to talk about it-

"Daddy was sloppy drunk and I could've stopped him but I went along with it." She wailed in self condemnation.

It was then that Chris got an understanding of what had transpired and immediately went into another level of love and a determination not to judge her.

"Have you told anybody else?" Douglas asked her.

She shook her head.

"What you just told us won't leave this room and what you do about Jerry is between you two but what we're concerned about is you havin' suicidal thoughts again because of this." Douglas told her.

"But how did you know?" She insisted as she sat there slowly rocking back and forth as if she was in physical pain while Chris stayed close by with one arm around her shoulder.

"Do you remember when we were talkin' in here this afternoon about how real God is?" Chris asked her.

She nodded slightly.

"He's real and we realize that you know that but sometimes He has a way of lettin' other people know what's goin' on so you can get some help." Douglas told her. "And we're not lookin' at you from some high pedestal or whatever because every one of us has a story and there's nothin' too big or hard for the blood of Jesus to cover, I don't care what it is."

"Even this?"

"Even this and this is what Calvary was all about and even though we know about it, we're not the ones that can do anything about it." "All we can do is let you know that there's a way to get this off of you and it's up to you what you do with it." Douglas told her.

"Is this what Janice was tryin' to tell me about in here when I was talkin' to her?"

"What did she say to you?" Chris asked.

"She told me about some things that happened around here that let her know that there was really somethin' to what everybody was always talkin' about." Marie answered after a moment.

"And she probably couldn't really explain to you what happened to her last week because you can't put into words what it feels like to have the power of God's spirit come into your physical body." Douglas said. "It blew my mind as hard as I thought I was but this is what God promised us because He knew that we couldn't do this on our own."

"So that's why she looks and sounds so different from what she was at home?" Marie asked as she kept wiping tears from her face.

"That's exactly why and she's still a spiritual newborn so she's probably still tryin' to process what happened but she was ready for it."

"She told me that after she saw what happened at the hospital the night of the accident with you and Kathryn that that's what did it." Chris said as she gave Marie another tissue. "That was what made her want the Holy Ghost and it takes different things for everybody but the end result is what matters."

"That was called doin' what you have to do."

"She told me about what mother did to you too and I apologize for her." Marie said.

"But I'm over it and I've moved on because if I kept dwellin' on that, it was just bring me down and I refuse to go there."...

CHAPTER 8

APRIL 1, WEDNESDAY

"Jerry went back home last night, he had to go back to work today." Marie remarked Wednesday afternoon as she, Irene and Janice stepped into the parking garage elevator at the hospital.

"Did he get a chance to come up here before he left?" Irene asked her.

She shook her head. "He stayed with his mother for two days and I've been with Aunt Frances so figure that one out." She said irritably. "And Irene you probably don't know how lucky you are to have such a sweet husband, don't ever take him for granted." She added as she remembered Sunday's experience with a small sense of relief as well as regret.

"Other people have told me that same thing so I don't but it hasn't always been like it is now, we had some serious issues right around the time he got himself together and we almost broke up."

"Are you serious?" Marie asked her in disbelief.

"It was bad and when we have more time I can tell you more about it but don't ever think that it can't be fixed." Irene told her as she sensed the tension in her voice at the subject of Jerry.

"I'll deal with one thing at a time." She abruptly said as she mentally reminded herself that this would be her first visit with Kathryn since the accident as they approached the floor where her room was. As she began to think of how hard it would be to face her with the knowledge of what had happened between her and Roy, she became almost physically ill and began looking for the nearest restroom.

"She's in room two twelve, we'll be in there." Janice told her as she and Irene started down the hallway.

"I really don't think that I can do this Chris and I'm sorry for botherin' you but it is what it is." She said a minute later as she sat on a chair in the restroom after calling her.

"You're not botherin' me Marie, I'm foldin' clothes." "But you really don't have much of a choice honey, she's probably wonderin' where you are so all you can do is forget about yourself for a minute and concentrate on doin' what you can for her." Chris told her. "She's really gonna be dependin' on you and Janice right through here so just take it one step at a time and it might not be as bad as you think."

"You haven't said anything about it to anybody else have you?"

"There's no way Marie, don't you remember what Douglas said about that?"

"Yeah I do but stuff happens, you know what I mean?"

"I know what you mean but put that out of your mind, it's not goin' anywhere else so just go in there and do what you have to do, this is gonna be okay because we're prayin' about it."

"Okay Chris, I'll let you know how it goes." "Love you." She added before ending the call.

"There you are, what took you so long?" Kathryn asked her five minutes later as she cautiously walked into the room.

"I was in the restroom." She said as she approached her wheelchair next to the bed and gave her a quick hug. "You look like you feel pretty good." She added as she sat on the side of her bed.

"I'm a lot better than I was this time a week ago but I still have a long way to go before I can get out of here." She said after a moment. "They just told me this mornin' that I'm gonna have to do six weeks of rehab because my right hip was dislocated so this is where I'll be for awhile" She added.

"You're not in any pain are you?" Irene asked her.

"If I am I don't know about it." She said, managing to laugh a little before turning her attention back to Marie. "And nobody has really told me what happened to your daddy Marie." She told her. "When I left him he was fine and then I get this news that he died in his sleep right before he was supposed to get here to see about me."

"That's what happened, I went over there Monday afternoon on my lunch break to drop somethin' off and I told him that I would be back Tuesday mornin' to take him to the airport." She began. "And when I called to make sure that he was ready to go, he wasn't answerin' the phone so I went over there and he wasn't comin' to the door." She said, starting to break down once again as she started to relive the moment that she had discovered his death, the day after her seemingly unpardonable act.

"Was it a heart attack?" Kathryn asked her.

"It probably was mother, I don't know." She told her. "This is the program from his funeral if you want it but I don't need to talk about it anymore." She added after getting it from her purse and handing it to her. "I'm done." She said as she got up to leave. "I am done."

"How's she doin' sweetheart?" Frances asked her an hour later after Irene brought her back.

"She's okay and we just found out that she's gonna be in rehab for another six weeks so I need to see about rentin' a car, I can't be dependin' on everybody else to take me out there every other day." She said wearily as she sat down across from her at the breakfast nook. "And Irene said to tell you that she'll see you at church tonight."

"Sheila got her new car yesterday so I have to ride with her tonight so I can check it out."

"What's goin' on tonight?"

"Just bible class from seven to nine and if you don't want to be here by yourself you might as well go with us."

"I might, Jerry said he might call and we really do need to work out some stuff." She made up as an excuse.

"Are you sure about that or is it that you just don't feel like it honey?" She asked her. "You don't have to pretend with me, I can tell when somethin' else is on your mind."

"I was just thinkin' about some stuff that I heard Douglas talkin' about the other night and I can only take so much at a time." She said after a moment.

"He can get a little intense but that's because the Lord saved him from so much and anytime he gets a chance to tell anybody about salvation, he's gonna do it with everything he has in him, bless his heart."

"And I told Irene not to ever take him for granted because there are so many couples that I know about that're hangin' on by a thread, includin' me."

"And I can remember when she was ready to walk out on him and not look back just because God got his attention one night and he got himself together in a big way."

"She told me that too and when you look at them now, that just seems impossible to me."

"I think when she realized that he wasn't gonna be playin' church and that he was goin' on with or without her, that's when she got her own revelation and she let God help her, as I like to tell my kids." She said, laughing a little. "And when you let God help you, you don't have any choice but to come out on top."

"But when you have somebody that is impatient and selfish and all of that kind of thing, you do things that you wouldn't otherwise." She said as she struggled to fight off thoughts and images that continued to haunt her. "What I did Sunday night was just not me aunt Frances and I don't understand how I got to that point."

"You got to that point because there is somethin' in you that wants and needs help to get out of your desperation honey." "And all of us have been there at one time or another and there's a place in the bible that calls it your wit's end."

"There's just too many things goin' on at once and when I try to sort stuff out, somethin' else always happens and I got to the place where I just couldn't deal anymore."

"And every one of us has stuff to deal with but the difference is havin' the spirit of God to get you through things." Frances told her. "And when Janice got to the place where she was almost goin' crazy, she pretty much gave it up and gave it all to God and that's when she got her help." "The Holy Ghost fell on her and she hasn't been the same since and that's what it's supposed to do, it makes you a new creature as the scripture says."

"Do you mind if I ask you somethin'?" She asked her after a moment. "And if you don't wanna talk about it, I understand, but where is Uncle William?"

"Honey you tell me and we'll both know." She said. "He has been comin' and goin' ever since Donna was about six months old and every now and then, he'll show up and ask about the kids and the next thing I know, he's gone again."

"He's been doin' that for twenty five or thirty years and you're still married to him?" She asked, shocked.

"Legally we are but I wouldn't call it a marriage, would you?" Frances asked her. "And because it's been like this for so long, there's not a lot of love lost, you see what I'm sayin'?" Frances asked her. "He wasn't here when I really could've used his help when Irene was off into another world with Douglas but it was situations like that that taught me how to get in touch with God."

"What could he have done though, she was grown."

"She was eighteen or nineteen when she met him but she was still at home and I'll never forget the first time he came to pick her up." She began. "He walked up to the front door behind this beard and dark glasses, smellin' like weed and tobacco and alcohol, all mixed up together and I almost had a heart attack."

"You are kiddin' me." Marie said in shock.

"He looks at me and says, I'm here for Irene, where is she?" "He didn't tell me what his name was and he was on this motorcycle that sounded like it needed two mufflers." She said, pausing to laugh. "It was a scary thing but because William wasn't there, I didn't have any choice but to learn how to depend on God."

"So you practically raised them by yourself."

"I did but every now and then he would send me a check but I ended up on food stamps and public assistance and all of that but we got through it." She said, reflecting back. "But what made you ask about him?"

"I was just wonderin' how you're makin' it because you don't let anything upset you, not even the way things turned out with you and him."

"Because it's a God thing honey, the Holy Ghost is a comforter, even in situations like that that I've gone through for over forty years." She immediately answered her. "The testimonies that I have are priceless and if I can help somebody else that might be goin' through some of the same things that I have, it's all worth it."

"And you're not bitter because of the way he just up and left you with four kids to raise by yourself?" She said, becoming angry at the thought.

"I could be but what would that change?" "I can't afford to put my soul in jeopardy by lettin' myself get caught up in hatred for him because that's how the devil gets the victory and that's not happenin.'"

"That is just so deep to me Aunt Frances." Marie said, shaking her head a little.

"It probably does sound that way to you but when you let the Lord help you, things work out for your good, even though a lot of time might go by." She said. "I've told the kids the same thing and they've been blessed because they haven't let themselves resent him."

"How long has it been since you've seen him?"

"He showed up here one day about three years ago and asked me how I was doin' and left a check for five hundred dollars in the mailbox and I haven't heard from him since."

"And you're okay with that?" She asked in amazement.

"It's not somethin' that I'm okay with but it's pretty much out of my hands and when God gets ready to step in and do whatever He chooses to do, I have to make myself content and be thankful that it's not any worse than it is."

"So you've been able to forgive him for all the years that he's done this to you, no questions asked?" She asked with skepticism.

"Don't have any choice honey because if I don't, I can't expect forgiveness for myself from the Lord and that's just the way it works." She said "And as hard as that might sound to you, it's not when you do it God's way, even if it seems to not make any sense."

To that, she had no answer as her mind kept taking her back in mental anguish at what she had allowed herself to do in the weakest moments of her life. She then began to recall the words that Douglas had ministered to her a few nights before about the cleansing power of the shed blood of Jesus and allowed herself to be moved at the very thought of being forever free of her guilt.

"Honey whatever it is that has you so worked up is not too big for the Lord to handle and you need to let us help you." Frances told her then as she noticed her begin to wince through her tears, right before her phone rang. When she noticed the call from Chris, she quickly got up and went to another room to answer it.

"I was fryin' chicken and it just came to me to call you." Chris told her after she answered. "How did it go?"

"Can you talk?"

"Yeah I can, what's goin' on?" She asked as she noticed the stress in her voice.

"I was in there talkin' to your mom and somethin' she said just set this off in me and I just can't shake this Chris."

"You didn't tell her did you?"

"I didn't but she can tell that I'm stressin' out and she keeps tellin' me that I need to let you guys help me but I can't tell anybody else what's goin' on with me." "You and Douglas are enough and I don't feel comfortable callin' him, I don't know him like that and he is somebody else's husband, you know what I'm sayin' Chris?"

"Yeah I can see how you feel like that but if he knew how much this is eatin' at you, he would probably stop what he was doin' to see what he could do for you." Chris told her. "But this is one of those things that only the Lord can fix; we can only go so far and when it comes down to it, this is between you and God and when you make a move to get this right and out of your life, He's gonna be there like yesterday Marie."

She didn't respond but continued to listen to her as she sat down on the bed in the guest room with the door closed.

"But I'm gonna call Douglas and see if he'll meet you at church tonight before bible class and you can come with Sheila and mother so you don't have to worry about callin' anybody for a ride." Chris told her. "He opens the buildin' up around six-thirty so that wouldn't be a problem so if that sounds okay to you, I'll call him now and let him know."

"If you're sure that it won't be a problem with him, okay." She said reluctantly.

"It won't be, he'll be glad to see you there."

"When Chris called me I told Irene that I was meetin' you here and she wanted me to tell you that she's prayin' for you." Douglas told Marie as he unlocked the Sunday school room across from the sanctuary two hours later.

"I need it." She said as she sat down.

"We all do and it's good that you realize what's goin' on because this is how you get your help from God." He told her. "You can't undo what went on but do you remember what we talked about Sunday night?" He asked her as he handed her a tissue from a nearby box.

"That's all I can think about except for when I keep seein' that day over and over again and I don't understand how I let myself go that low Douglas." She said in desperation.

"And that's exactly why the Lord promised us the Holy Ghost because He knows that this flesh that we're all livin' in has the potential to go that low as you put it." He told her with emphasis. "We were all born with the ability to do whatever the devil brings to our mind and without the Spirit of God, we don't have the power not to do, even when we don't want to do." He added as he did his best to "break it down".

She nodded a little as she kept her face covered with the tissue.

"Marie come here for a second." He told her as he helped her to stand back up.

Without resistance she followed him into the sanctuary and sat down on a back row pew.

"What does that say up there?" He asked her, referring to the scripture Acts2:38 that was painted behind the baptismal pool:

"Then Peter said unto them, Repent and be baptized every one of you in the name of Jesus Christ for the remission of sins and ye shall receive the gift of the Holy Ghost." She read slowly as uncontrollable tears fell when she began to feel the anointing of God behind the scripture.

"You're believin' that aren't you?" Douglas asked as he sat down in the pew in front of her.

She nodded as she continued to allow him to patiently work with her and to help her to get an understanding of what she had just read.

"None of us can force you or talk you into anything, this is somethin' that you're gonna have to make up in your mind that you want for yourself." "This is your salvation and when you get to the place where nothin' else matters, you'll do whatever it takes because there's not anything that's more serious than eternity." He concluded as he noticed her countenance change as she stared straight ahead to the scripture, repeatedly reading it while taking in everything he said to her.

"How come I've never heard of this before, I used to go to church all of the time and nobody has ever talked about this."

"I can't really give you an honest answer to that because the first time I ever set foot in a church was when I came in here fifteen years ago." "But this is not new, the Holy Ghost first fell over two-thousand years ago and one of the best, most powerful things about this is the justification that happen once you come up out of that water after the name of Jesus is spoken over you". "Anything and everything you've ever done wrong is gone, just as if you never did any of it and it's all because of the blood of Jesus."

At that she quickly got up and walked out, totally overcome at the very thought of what her heart had just comprehended. Then as Sheila and Frances came in the door and noticed her out in the hallway, searching for the restroom Sheila quickly went to her side and guided her back into the sanctuary where it was beginning to fill up.

"Can you get me up there?" She asked Sheila, nearly pleading with her.

"She's there." Douglas told Sheila then as she looked at him not quite understanding what she meant until he motioned her towards the baptism pool.

"Honey what in the world did you say to her?" Frances asked him five minutes later as she sat down next to him.

"Justification." Was all he could say as they watched a church minister step down into the water to wait for Marie. "Is Janice here yet?" He asked her as he took a handkerchief from his pocket. "I don't want her to miss this."

"They're probably on their way." She said, putting an arm around him as she noticed how overcome he had become at what was happening at the moment, coupled with what he had seen and heard over the previous three days. This was the result of fervent effectual and intercessory prayer, conceived out of love for the soul crying out for help and now receiving it through faith and obedience to the Word of God.

"Is somebody gettin' baptized?" Janice asked then as she walked into the sanctuary with Chris and Patti.

"Guess who honey." Frances told her as someone stood up and started to sing the song "Glory to His Name" as Marie was assisted down into the pool by the minister.

Then without saying another word she and Chris stood there and cried together as they recognized her before the minister spoke the words of baptism over her:

"And now my dearly beloved, upon the confession of your faith and the confidence that you have in the Word of God, concerning the Death, Burial and Resurrection of Jesus Christ, I now baptize you in the name of Jesus, for the remission of sin and with a repentant heart, you shall receive the gift of the Holy Ghost." "In Jesus name" he repeated with emphasis as he submerged her into the water. Then as she was brought back up, both of her hands went up as she let out a shrill scream before she began to speak in a tongue not her own as the spirit of God gave her utterance, as evidence that the Holy Ghost had taken up residence in her being.

Then through her rejoicing, Chris began to video on her phone as the church "went up" in response to this new birth unlike any other experience, defying description. As Marie continued to submit herself to the spirit of God by "letting it happen", Douglas, Frances and Janice sat in their seats, "crying like babies" at the faithfulness of God and His Word, that can never be broken.

"As many times as I have been to church, I have never heard the truth like this, this is unreal, oh my God." Marie managed to say two hours later as she sat in the sanctuary with Irene, Chris and Janice. "I can't believe that this is me." She added as she tried to still herself.

"It's you, believe it, but what I need to know is what it was that made such a difference so quick." Chris told her as they sat waiting on James and Douglas in a meeting. "When I talked to you on the phone, you sounded like stress times two."

"When we got here, Douglas was waitin' in the parkin' lot and he took me in one of those rooms over there and he just started breakin' it all down so I would really understand what was goin' on." She began tearfully. "And then we came in here and he had me read that scripture up there." She said pointing to it while trying to compose herself as she thought back to the moment. "But what really blew my mind was when he told me that anything and everything I've ever done wrong would be gone; history." She added, waving her hand in a swiping motion. "Oh my God." She said again as if it were too much to believe.

"That is some powerful stuff Marie, keep goin.'" "I am lovin' this." Chris told her.

"Then it was like somethin' actually got me up and I ended up out there in the hall and there was Sheila comin' in the front door, out of nowhere." She recalled. "And I don't know whether she could tell that I didn't know where I was or what was happenin', but she brought me back in here and I think I remember hearin' Douglas say she's there, whatever that meant."

"He could tell that you were ready."

She nodded a little. "I was and she took me back there and showed me where to change and you know the rest." She said as James and Douglas came back into the sanctuary from the meeting. Then as she immediately got up and went towards them, there was an unspoken understanding between them as she embraced both of them individually while she thought of the moment that they had seen her at her worse, but were now witnessing the result of the powerful name of Jesus, only three days later.

"This is your new start so don't let anything or anybody mess this up for you." Douglas told her. "And if you don't remember anything else, always let God help you."...

CHAPTER 9

APRIL 5, SUNDAY

"Aunt Frances had me cookin' yesterday because this is the first Sunday of the month and everybody ends up over here." Marie commented at the breakfast nook with Irene, Douglas and Janice Sunday afternoon.

"This is somethin' that she started about ten years ago so she could keep up with everything and everybody and it stuck." Irene said. "But I told her that once James and Paul get their houses built out there, we need to start goin' out to the country because it's startin' to be too many for this house."

"So are they gonna be buildin' both houses at the same time?" Marie asked as she poured iced tea in a glass.

"Chris and James have a contractor but he's got about twenty people from church that volunteered to do Jane and Paul's." Douglas said. "That's what the meetin' was about Wednesday night."

"I called Jerry last night and I was tryin' to explain to him what happened to me Wednesday night and I just couldn't think of the right words." Marie said, shaking her head a little.

"You can't explain it because it's not like anything else you can compare it to." Douglas said. "I tried to do the same thing and I started tellin' people that you have to get it for yourself to really understand it."

"Is he gonna be able to take off so he can come back here for a minute?" Janice asked her.

"I asked him about that and he has a couple of weeks that he can use but he's not sure when he can actually take off." "And I told mother that we would probably be out there sometime today to see her."

"When are they startin' her rehab stuff?' Irene asked.

"Tomorrow and she wants one of us to be there with her because she doesn't really understand what they're gonna be doin.'"

"Does she know about you yet?"

"I tried to tell her too but it was a lost cause." She said as Patti walked in the kitchen from the dining room.

"Daddy said to give you this." She said as she handed Douglas a folded insurance form for him to examine. "Are you okay now?" She asked Marie as she remembered what had happened the week before.

"Sweetheart I'm more than okay now and I didn't get a chance to thank you for what you did." She told her. "Can I get a hug?" Marie asked her after a moment.

She nodded as she came towards her and allowed her to give her a heartfelt embrace.

"I'm gonna cry." Janice said after she ran back out a moment later. "That was so sweet of her." She added as she got a napkin from the holder. "And I haven't said anything about this before now but right before she started down the steps, she said that an angel told her to go downstairs." She added.

"Are you serious Janice?" Irene asked her. "That sounds like one of those things mother used to tell us about that gives you the chills, like now."

"Why should you have the chills, you know this stuff is real honey." Douglas told her. "And that just proves that the Lord uses kids to help us out because somewhere we lose that kind of faith." "My Lord." He added as he passed Marie a napkin.

"Did she say what it looked like?" Irene asked, fascinated.

"We were talkin' about it the next day because I just wanted to make sure she was okay and she said like it wasn't a big deal, that angel told her to go downstairs." Janice said, remembering the conversation. "The kids were out in the hallway playin' and I was in our room with 'Nita and she just got up all of a sudden like and went downstairs."

"Is it enough food back here for everybody?" Frances asked as she came in with an empty coffee pot.

"Yeah it is, and we were just talkin' about you and your stories that give you the chills." Douglas told her.

"Like the night I got off the bus up the street about a block and a half away and this was probably about nine-thirty or ten o' clock." She began as she sat down in a chair at the end of the table. "And I think it was Donna that had been watchin' out this window right here and when I came in the door she asked me who those two men were that I was walkin' down the street with." "Then I looked at her and said that I was by myself, there weren't two men with me and she had details about how they looked." She recalled. "And then I thought about it later, and it came to me that what she saw must've been a couple of angels that were invisible to me but anybody else that was around that time of night that wanted to try somethin' crazy wouldn't do anything because of these two men that were with me."

"That is so deep Aunt Frances, I'm sittin' here trippin' off of that." Janice told her.

"But you would tell us all of the time that angels were here with us in the house watchin' over us when you couldn't be here." Irene told her.

"Every time I would have to leave for somethin', that's what I'd say and nothin' ever happened to you either." She said as Douglas got up to answer his phone.

"Michael Johnson, speak to me." He spoke to his younger brother from St. Louis.

"Hey, what's up man, you probably wasn't expectin' to hear from me today were you?"

"And that makes me think that somethin' is wrong, is everybody okay?"

"Yeah we're makin' it okay." He said with hesitation. "Irene and the kids doin' alright?"

"They're all good, but you need to cut to the chase Michael, what's goin' on?" "I haven't known you all of your life for nothin.'"

88

"I just got laid off man and I've got to find another job, like yesterday."

"You were still with the phone company?"

"I was but since nobody has land lines anymore, they cut half of the factory staff down here and I just need to start over somewhere else."

"Are you willin' to do somethin' altogether different or do you want the same kind of thing?"

"As long as it's a job that's not in trouble or layin' off, I'm ready to do whatever it takes to keep a paycheck comin' in." He said with desperation. "And this minimum wage stuff is a joke, don't even go there with me."

"How long have you been laid off?"

"A couple of weeks and I've been on line almost twenty four seven tryin' to find somethin' but I'm not gettin' anywhere down here." He concluded. "So if you know of anything up there, I can be there by this time tomorrow if that wouldn't be a problem."

"Give me a couple of days to look around and I'll talk to Irene about you stayin' with us for a minute 'til you find somethin.'"

"Man I appreciate you doin' that and if you come up with somethin', call or text me and I can get up there real quick if that's what it takes."

"I've never been to a church before where you can actually feel God and I really don't know where to go once I get back home." Marie commented as Douglas came back in and sat down. "And it almost makes me not want to go back because of that."

"What would Jerry think about that?" Frances asked her.

"I wouldn't even try that unless he would go along with it but it might not be that hard to do because his mother is here." She said after a moment.

"But Kathryn would have a hard time with both of her girls leavin' her there by herself so just start now tryin' to find somewhere in D.C. that does it like the bible says." Frances told her. "And don't settle for anywhere that doesn't because you know for yourself now what the difference is."

"When I talked to Jerry the other day, he could tell that I sounded different from the way I did the last time he called."

"And when he sees you again it'll be the same thing." Douglas told her. "But what you don't need to do is try to convince him of anything with a lot of talk because that has the opposite effect, believe me." He said as he nudged Irene. "Let your life do your talkin.'"

"He's signifyin' but that's true." Irene said. "The night he got the Holy Ghost, he came home and started tryin' to tell me that I had to get it too and that just ticked me off even more." "I was horrible." She added, laughing at herself. "And I knew he was right but I wasn't gonna give him the satisfaction by admittin' it."

"But why weren't you glad about it, this is a huge deal." Marie asked her.

"I knew that our lifestyle was about to change and I thought we were havin' a good time out there runnin' with the world and I had a real problem with it." She said, thinking back. "But after a while, I could tell that all of my fussin' and gripin' about it wasn't doin' a thing and I saw that Junkyard wasn't nowhere to be found." She continued. "I would do things that I thought would make him cuss me out and nothin' I did worked." "I was crazy when I think about it." She added in hindsight.

"The Holy Ghost did some kind of job on this man, you hear me?" Frances asked as she took his hand and squeezed it. "And I know that we talk about it over and over again but the Lord doesn't want us to ever forget about the places and the things that He rescued us from because it could've been so different."

"Here I go again, I can't stand it." Janice said as she wiped tears from her face.

"You go right ahead honey, you have a right to rejoice as much as somebody that's had the Holy Ghost for fifty years because he ordered your steps and allowed all of this to happen to you for a reason."

"And this is for both of you because you're new babies and the sooner you get a relationship with the Lord, the better off you'll be." Douglas told them. "Things will happen to you that will try your faith in God but you have what it takes to overcome yourself and He gave you His spirit to help keep you out of trouble and it works if you allow it to."

"But don't be surprised when you have times where you just don't understand what's goin' on but stay on your knees because there's not anything that you can't talk to the Lord about." Frances commented. "And we're not talkin' to you like this to discourage you or make you think that you made a mistake by lettin' the Lord save you, but you need to be taught that you're gonna have problems to deal with like everybody else, but the difference is that you have power now that you didn't have before to get over things that're gonna be part of life 'til Jesus comes."

"I wasn't thinkin' that way at all and I'm glad that you guys are tellin' us things because we just didn't hear the truth at home like this." Marie said. "It was like you could do anything you wanted to do and still be okay because God understands why you did it and all of that but now that I see that it's a little deeper than that, it makes so much difference."

"And that's because you're lettin' your Holy Ghost show you things that you didn't understand before now." Douglas told her. "And there are things about all of us that need to be perfected and overcome and that's all a part of what holiness is about." "You might get tempted to do some things that you know are wrong but that's where your power comes in and it works if you let it."

"Do you remember that pack of cigarettes you found in that leather jacket a couple of years ago?" Irene asked him.

"You know I do." He said, shaking his head a little. "I was goin' through some old stuff for the Goodwill bag one day and I was makin' sure that there wasn't any money left in the pockets."

"And there they were." Marie said, finishing his sentence.

"And there they were you're right." He said, agreeing with her. "And to this day, I don't understand how I missed that one pack of cigarettes when I was gettin' rid of all of the other stuff that I had been caught up in out there." He continued. "But I heard this voice in my head that said, just one won't hurt you and it was as clear as if somebody was standin' right next to me tryin' to make me take a few more puffs."

"Sounds like a devil's imp to me." Frances said, laughing a little.

"Whether it was that or my old mind, it didn't matter and my point is that nobody is above temptation but I wasn't goin' there with the smokes as we used to call 'em." "By that time I had found out just how powerful the Holy Ghost is and it wasn't hard to throw 'em in the garbage can, but it was somethin' about the scent of the tobacco that just brought it all back and made me that much more thankful that the Lord did what He does best."

"Don't be leavin' me out of this bible class goin' on back here." Sheila said, coming back into the kitchen with a plate.

"We're just talkin' to the babies, they need to hear a few things from folks that have been through a few things." Frances said.

"What time are you goin' to the hospital?" She asked Marie.

"Probably around five or six, are you goin' with us?"

"I haven't gotten a chance to talk to her since the accident and I don't want her to think that I've forgotten about her." She said as she got a chicken leg from the platter on the stove. "Two weeks is long enough."

"Do you think that he would come up here so I can talk to him?" Kathryn asked as she slowly walked down the hospital hall way with the aid of a walker with Janice and Marie on either side of her an hour later.

"Do you want one of us to ask him?" Marie asked, referring to Douglas. "He probably doesn't have time tonight but maybe sometime this week he might be able to come up here."

"I really do need to see him because of what happened right before this accident and sometimes I feel like I brought this on myself."

"He's probably not thinkin' about that anymore mother; he said he's over it." Janice told her.

"He might be but I'm not and I need to get with him as soon as I can." She said impatiently. "I feel like I won't get any better until I talk to him because I owe him an apology." She continued. "I lost your father on top of all of this and God is punishing me."

"How come you're thinkin' like this all of a sudden?" Marie asked her. "You need to be concentratin' on gettin' better instead of worryin' about stuff like that." She added as they approached her room where Sheila was waiting on them.

"Hey Aunt Kathryn, I didn't know I was gonna see you walkin' around." Sheila said as she got up to give her a hug.

"I'm barely walkin' but this is progress I guess."

"You look a lot different than you did the last time I was up here." Sheila told her. "And I don't even think you knew that I was in the room."

"How did you come out without a scratch and I'm in here like this?" She said as she slowly sat down on the side of her bed.

"We got hit on your side but just be glad it wasn't as bad as they said it was."

"They didn't think you were gonna make it through that first night so you have God to thank that you're still here." Janice told her with loving respect.

"Honey you don't have to start preachin' to me because if it wasn't for you, I wouldn't be in this shape." She said as her mood suddenly changed for no apparent reason. "And it's startin' to show now so you can't hide it anymore."

At that last comment Janice refused to react to her "fiery dart" that was intended to cause an atmosphere of strife and division between them.

"I love you too mother and I know that it's startin' to come out but it's there and I can't do anything but let God help me with this just like He's helpin' you." She said calmly.

"Do you need us to bring you anything before we leave?" Marie asked her, purposely changing the subject.

"I need to be by myself for a while." "But I still want you to tell what's his name to come up here and talk to me before I change my mind." She said irritably as she lay back down on the bed. "And tell him to call before he comes.".

APRIL 7, TUESDAY

"I got the message from Sheila Sunday night at church and she made sure I knew that she was serious as a heart attack." Douglas remarked Tuesday afternoon at the kitchen table with Chris and Michael.

"Janice told me how she sort of turned on her when they were at the hospital but that's another story, I'll talk to you about it later." She said as she set two glasses of ice in front of them. "So when did you get here Michael?"

"Last night around eight 'o clock." "It took me about four hours to get here."

"Did you know that if you had a beard you could pass for twins?" "It's almost scary, you look exactly like Douglas did ten years ago."

"I've heard that but our personalities are nothin' alike."

"Is that a good or a bad thing?" She asked him as she handed him a can of pop.

"I'd better quit while I'm ahead."

"What time do Janice and James usually get here?" Douglas asked after opening his laptop.

"They get off at three so they're on their way." "Is this the homeowner's insurance application?"

"Yeah we need all of the raw numbers like square feet and good stuff like that." "Does he have the blueprint here?"

"It's in his office over there but some of this I already know without lookin' at it like the number of bedrooms and bathrooms." She said, as she read the screen after he turned it towards her.

"Let me take a guess, five bedrooms, and four bathrooms?"

"He must've already told you, that was too slick Douglas."

"He tells me everything as long as it's not too personal."

"How many kids do you have?" Michael asked her.

"Seven." "Four boys and three girls."

"You don't look like you've had that many kids, what're you doin' right?"

"I don't have a lot of time to be sittin' around so that keeps me sort of in shape." She said as James and Janice came in the back door.

"Check this out, company." James said.

"You're right on time, we're workin' up your stuff." Douglas told him as Janice gave him a quick hug. "Hey hon."

"Michael this is James, James this is Michael." Chris said as she quickly introduced them. "And this is Janice my cousin." She added as she noticed him staring intently at her.

"You didn't tell me everything did you?" Michael asked Douglas a moment later after James went to his office for the blueprint.

"Probably because I didn't think about it." Douglas said as he kept working on the form.

"I'm sorry Chris, I just didn't have any warnin.'" He told her.

"You don't have to be sorry, we are so used to that that we don't even think about it."

"And he'll tell you in a minute that he's not what he looks like." Douglas said.

"So your cousin works with him or somethin'?"

"Yeah she moved here from D.C. a few months ago and she needed a job and it just sort of worked out."

"Has he got any more connections?"

"He's about to build my brother's house so if you know anything about that kind of stuff, he might be able to use you."

"Ask him about it Michael, he won't bite you." Douglas told him.

"They're brothers, he has three sisters so James adopted him." Chris said as she nudged him.

"I'm just not used to seein' so much warm and fuzzy stuff goin' on, I feel like I'm in a Hallmark movie or somethin.'" Michael said, laughing a little.

"Where else have you been, did you take him to meet mother?" Chris asked.

"Yeah we stopped over there for a few minutes before we got here and he got one of her hugs like she hadn't seen him in twenty years." Douglas said.

"How do you that, she doesn't know me from the man in the moon."

"That doesn't matter, you're Douglas' brother and she's in love with him so end of subject." Chris said.

"It's not so much that, she loves how the Lord got a hold of me and set my feet on straight street." He said, quoting the words from the songs. "And that's okay, it doesn't hurt to have somebody keep you in line like she does."

"But she's still in love with you, admit it." She said as James came back in.

"Man I apologize, nobody told me and I was shocked for a second." Michael told him.

"No problem, I'm not what I look like." He said as he handed Douglas the print. "So you're here lookin' for a job?" He asked him as he sat down next to Chris.

"Yeah pretty much, I gave up on St. Louis so this might work out but I won't know 'til I try." He said after a moment. "And Chris told me that you're about to build a house."

"Seven thousand square feet so the more hands we have the quicker we can get it done." He said. "And Paul called me this mornin' and told me that Jane's mother is buyin' their house for rental property because she's tired of waitin' on another buyer."

"Are you serious?" Chris asked, shocked.

"Remember when we prayed over this project Wednesday night?" Douglas asked him.

"Yeah I do but I didn't think things would start happenin' this quick." James said as he noticed the look of confusion from Michael.

"Okay, help me out." "Is it one or two houses goin' up?"

"What happened was my brother's mother-in-law bought them four acres out in the country about ten miles from here and they're splittin' it with us." Chris told him. "He said that he doesn't want to have to take care of all of that land by himself so they get two and we get two."

"So you're buildin' and so is your brother so there's two houses goin' up at the same time.

"You got it but we're havin' ours done by a contractor and the church is doin' theirs."

"I think I got it now and you need a couple more hands to help build the bigger one, the seven thousand square foot one." Michael said after thinking a moment. "Have you already sold this one?"

"My sister and her husband are buyin' it, we're closin' in about a month."

"So how many kids does your brother have?" "That's a lot of room so I'm gonna guess nine or ten."

"We'll let him tell you, I'll just say they have enough to fill it up." Chris told him.

"How soon can you start?" James asked him. "Since she's probably already cut him a check, we can get started some time next week but if you find somethin' else in the meantime, don't let this stop you from takin' a another job."

"I don't have anything but time so that's not a problem, just let me know when you need me."

"This happened Sunday when her and Marie went out there to see her?" Douglas asked Chris ten minutes later after James took Michael back to his home office.

She nodded. She said that all of a sudden she started sayin' stuff like if it hadn't been for her she wouldn't be in the shape that she's in, and how she can't hide it anymore and mess like that."

"Yeah that's mess and she really does need to be careful about her choice of words because they have a way of comin' back to haunt you." Douglas said.

"Are you goin' out there to talk to her?" "You might as well go and see what's goin on with her because she'll keep bringin' it up 'til you do."

"I'm plannin' on it but either Marie or Janice needs to be there too because they need to see just how to handle her."

"How do you mean?"

"Sometimes when people start to go off out of the blue like that, there's a spirit behind it and they need to know how to use the power and the authority that they have to fight that craziness." Douglas said after thinking a moment before answering her.

"You're not playin' are you?"

"No ma'am I'm not and I don't say things like that off the top of my head either." "If they let that go on, the spirit behind that could eat them alive because they don't know exactly what they're dealin' with and I can't just sit back and let that happen."

"None of us can and what made it worse was the way Aunt Kathryn keeps remindin' her about how she's really startin' to show and she's already self conscious about it." Chris remarked. "And I don't know whether you noticed it or not but did you see the way Michael was checkin' her out when she came in here with James?"

"You know good and well that I noticed it and that's why she didn't hang around." "She noticed it too and that can be another devil's device that could throw her off track so you know I'm on top of that one don't you?"

"Yeah I can tell, I haven't known you all this time for nothin.'" She said, laughing at him.

"You already know so if you ever notice anymore red flags, you know my number and where I live and I'm gonna tell James the same thing." He told her.

"Do I see a little junkyard comin' out in you?"

"Junkyard would've grabbed him by his throat and cursed him out but you know I'm not goin' there." "My fights are won on my knees and this is just another thing to keep me humble, believe me when I tell you."...

CHAPTER 10

APRIL 10, FRIDAY

"So this is you and Chris' brother's place that we're headed to from here?" Michael asked as he and Irene fastened the twins into car seats Friday morning.

"Yeah his wife wants to take me out to the lot, I haven't seen it yet so we're followin' her out there before it rains."

"James told me how her mother did all of this for them because she thought they didn't have enough room where they are."

"They can use more room but it's not like they're on top of each other." "Jane thinks she's tryin' to make up for some stuff that she's said to her because of Paul but it really doesn't matter, everybody wins." Irene said as she started the van. "And James and Chris have opened up that house for a lot of people and this is their time to get it back."

"And they have seven of their own plus your other cousins stayin' there too?"

"Yeah but they're built in babysitters and housekeepers so it all works out."

"How old is the one that works with James?" He asked her cautiously. "What's her name, Janice?"

"She just turned eighteen in February."

"When I saw her the other day I noticed that her and Douglas seem to have a pretty good thing goin' on, what's up with that?"

"There's kind of a story behind that and it's one of those things that you might have to ask him about when you get a chance." Irene told him. "But her father died a couple of weeks ago and Douglas has sort of stepped in and taken his place if you wanna put it that way."

"Like I told them when I was over there the other day, I feel like I'm in a Hallmark movie around here."

"Is that good or bad?" Irene asked, laughing at him.

"I'm still tryin' to figure this out up here, am I in some kind of make believe world or somethin'?"

"How do you mean honey, explain that to me."

"I've been here since Tuesday and I haven't heard no yellin', no fussin' and cussin' out of anybody and it's like, are these people for real?" He began. "I have never had anybody hug me like your mother did the other day and she'd never seen me before in her life before Tuesday."

"But you're Douglas' brother and that goes a long way with her."

"That's what Chris said so it must be somethin' to it."

"That's just the way she is and when you get a chance to sit down and talk to her, it'll be like she's known you for years."

"I might have to do that, she seems to be pretty approachable." He remarked as they stopped at a traffic light. "And I wanted to talk to Janice the other day but she didn't give me a chance;she gave Douglas a hug and she was out of there."

"Chris said that she's really self conscious about her baby bump and maybe she just didn't feel comfortable stickin' around."

"She shouldn't be feelin' like that, she's a pretty girl and so what if she's pregnant." "This is not the fifties." He added with a hint of anger.

"It's not but some things don't change, even if the way people think have and she's not the type to be passin' it off like it's not a big deal."

"Is the baby's father around?"

Irene shook her head. "He's in D.C. somewhere so she's plannin' on handlin' things on her own." She said. "Did you still need to stop at the store up here, they have a hiring sign in the window." She asked him as she purposely steered the conversation away from Janice.

"Yeah why not, that would be better than nothin' at all." He said after a moment. "That lets you know how desperate I am."

"They are not playin' around are they, I didn't know that they had actually started on their house." Jane remarked an hour later as she, Irene and Michael walked around on the lot.

"They just broke ground on it last week but it looks like they've already gotten the basement done." Irene noticed as they stood back from the building site while she took pictures with her phone.

"So where does your place start?" Michael asked Jane as they slowly walked around the property.

"See where those flags are over there?" She asked, pointing to the area where they were set in rows. "Do you feel like walkin'?"

"Yeah I need to check out where I might be workin', James is pretty sure he might need some more help." He said as Irene caught up with them.

"I've got to go pick Gail up at school, she just threw up and I need to go get her." She told them.

"I'll ride back with her, I need to check this out." He told Irene.

"When did you talk to James about workin' out here?" Jane asked him a moment later as they walked toward the flags.

"I got here Tuesday and I went over there with Douglas and got the shock of my life when he walked in the door." He said, laughing a little.

"Douglas didn't tell you did he?"

"He said he didn't think about it but I got some warnin' about you so I wasn't surprised."

"Is that a big deal to you?"

"It's not a big deal but I've had a couple of major problems with a few people down in St. Louis and it's a trust issue, you know what I'm sayin'?"

"Yeah I do, that was my mother's problem when I married Paul and it's taken her this long to get over herself but my father never did." She said. "He would turn over in his grave if he knew that she was spendin' all of this money on his biracial grandkids, but God has a way of workin' things out when you keep doin' the right thing."

"So what did she do, just call you one day and say I found this property for sale and I bought it for you to build a new house on."

"That's pretty much what happened; we had talked about findin' a bigger place and we didn't tell her that but the Lord knew." She said, as she began to become overwhelmed at the thought.

"Did I hear that she's buyin' your old place for rental property because she got tired of waitin' on a buyer?"

"She called Paul Tuesday mornin' at work and told him that our house was sold because she had called our realtor and let him know that she was buyin' it." She said. "We close on the fifteenth and I think James said that there's no reason why they can't break ground on it that week-end."

"And he's havin' theirs built by a contractor so he can have the time to build yours?"

"He's got it like that as the kids say." "Janice told me how many clients he has just from referrals because his work is so good and that's why he's at a place where he can do that."

"Even though he has seven kids to feed with a wife that stays home." Michael said. "I don't understand how him and Douglas do it."

"It all goes back to trustin' God with what you have and managin' your money right and He can show you how to do it if you don't know how."

"I've got to find the job first then I'll worry about the rest of it."

"Did I tell you how much you remind me of Douglas when he was your age?"

"I've heard that a lot since I've been here but I don't think I'll ever be as successful as he is."

"But I remember him before he was able to do what he's doin' now so don't be discouraged by a couple of setbacks."

"That's easy to say if you're not the one dealin' with those setbacks and if somethin' doesn't happen pretty soon around here, it's not gonna be a pretty picture." He said. "And I don't know why I'm unloadin' on you like this, you don't know me from that rabbit over there."

"I don't have to know you to listen to you and if you're gonna be workin' on my house we have to start somewhere." She told him. "And like it or not, we're in this together so don't be scared to trust me."

"So if I tell you that I'm gonna go after Janice, I won't hear about it from somebody else around here?"

"That would be between you and her but if I were you, I wouldn't try that young man." She told him after a moment. "And I'm dead serious when I say that." She added, shaking her head.

"What's the problem with that?" "I liked what I saw the other day and I'm goin' after it." He repeated in a matter of fact way.

"Your brother is a prayin' man and nobody would have to say a word but he would be on that like yesterday." She warned him.

"Am I supposed to be afraid of that?" "I've known Douglas all of my life and he couldn't say much because back in the day he got what he wanted when he wanted it and nobody was puttin' the brakes on him if you know what I mean." "What could he say, Johnson men get what they want."

"I know exactly what you mean but she's gotten herself together and she is not doin' that anymore." "It might've been a little different if this was a couple of months ago but she's not goin' there now, believe me."

"We'll see about that and I had to get that out in the open and you just happened to be close by." He said with an arrogant tone. "We'll just see about that."

"We'll meet you up there hon, give me a minute or two." Douglas told Marie after she and Janice met him in the hospital lobby that evening.

"Am I in trouble?" She asked him a moment later as she sat back down.

"No ma'am, you're not in trouble, but I need to give you a heads up about Michael and I don't know if you noticed it the other day or not but he's probably gonna be comin' after you, let's just keep it real."

"I did notice that he was starin' like he was tryin' to figure me out or somethin' and that was why I went on upstairs."

"He was checkin' you out and Chris noticed it too so I'm just makin' sure that you know that that can't happen because you have the Holy Ghost now, and it's a whole new thing from what it was before."

"I thought that was the way it is but I wasn't sure." She said then after thinking a moment.

"You weren't sure because you haven't been taught that before now and I don't want you to feel bad or guilty because you didn't know." He told her. "And it's a good thing that you're sensitive to what the Lord is tellin' you because that's what's keepin' you out of trouble."

"I am so glad that you're talkin' to me like this because I really wasn't sure and I didn't know how to bring it up."

"And God knows that which is why He led me to take you aside like this to let you know what's goin' on." He told her. "And if you feel like you need to talk about this with somebody other than me, you can always go to Chris or Irene or even Sheila, she's closer to your age and she's good to talk to, so don't ever hesitate." "This is serious business and none of us go through here by ourselves so we do what we have to do to make it." He added. "So the bottom line, in holiness, sex is for married people."

She nodded a little. "But do you really think Michael would try that?" "He doesn't know me."

"He doesn't have to know you, he wants what he wants and when you're thinkin' like that, he'll do anything to try to break you down." "And I don't have to tell you what to say or do because you have some experience and you're not a twelve or thirteen year old kid that doesn't know what's goin' on." He said as he stood up. "And whatever you do, let God help you." He added as they started towards the elevator.

"I was about to give up on you, what took you so long to get up here?" Kathryn asked Douglas five minutes later as he and Janice walked into her room. "Were you down there talkin' about me behind my back?" She asked, joking in a serious way.

"You're lookin' like you feel a lot better than you did the last time I saw you." Douglas told her as he sat down, ignoring her comment.

"I do and we just found out that I'm gettin' out of here in a couple of days." She said.

"And I was really surprised when they said that it was okay for her to fly." Marie commented. "So that means we can get you back home."

"And Janice I still have your plane ticket if you're ready to go back with us." She told her.

She shook her head. "No ma'am, I don't have anything to go back there for." She said without hesitation. "This is where I need to be."

"What in the world have you been tellin' my daughter?" She asked Douglas then.

"Mother please don't get anything started, we have already been through all of that and she's not comin' back to D.C." Marie told her.

"If it makes you feel any better, we haven't been talkin' about that one way or the other." Douglas said. "And was there somethin' else you needed to talk to me about?" He asked her as he purposely took control of the conversation.

"I need for you to forgive me for what happened between you and me that night." She managed to say. "I didn't have the right to do that because you haven't done anything but help Janice since she's been here and I apologize." She added as let a couple of tears fall down her face before Marie handed her tissue.

"Sweetheart from this day on, we're gonna act like that never happened, so in other words, it's time to move on." He told her. "You're forgiven and as far as I'm concerned, it's over and done with and you need to forgive yourself too." He told her with heartfelt emphasis. "Don't keep beatin' yourself up about it because that doesn't do anything but make you feel worse."

She nodded a little as she reached out for one of his hands. "And I want you to promise me that you're gonna take care of Janice because Roy is gone and she needs a strong man to look out for her."

"We've already talked about that and we'll make sure that her and the baby are taken care of." He told her.

"Did you hear that Janice?" She asked her. "I want you to know how blessed you are to have him step in and do what he's doin' for you so don't ever take that for granted."

"I won't." She said as she struggled to keep it together.

"This accident that I was in made me see things a lot different than I did before and I feel like God is givin' me another chance to get things right". She continued. "And whatever I've said to you that might've hurt your feelings, I'm apologizin' to you too because I don't know when I'll see you again after we leave here in a couple of days."

"It's all okay mother, you don't have to keep goin' back to all of that anymore, I'm okay." She insisted. "I'll call you probably once a week and when the baby gets here, you might be able to come back and stay for a while." She added, attempting to reassure her.

"She'll be alright and if somethin' would happen, they would let us know." Marie told her. "She's in good hands, believe me."

"Have you heard from Jerry lately?" Douglas asked her.

"I talked to him a couple of days ago and he's ready for me to get back but I already know that there's gonna be some issues, sort of like you and Irene did, you know what I mean?"

"I know what you mean but that can be a good thing too." He told her. "It might look and feel like a hard situation but as long as you don't start takin' down and compromisin' you have the power to change things." He told her. "Are you doin' anything tomorrow night around six-thirty?"

"I haven't made any plans, what's goin' on?"

"We're havin' a youth get together and dinner and if you have the time, stop by because we need to see you before you leave."

"Sounds like a plan, we'll be there.".

APRIL 11, SATURDAY

"What time are you leavin, tomorrow night sometime?" Irene asked Saturday evening around six o' clock as Marie sat down at the kitchen table with a plate.

"Seven-thirty, Sheila's takin' us to the airport and in a way, I really hate to leave but life goes on as they say."

"Don't you miss Jerry?" "I know you do".

"I do but there's always gonna be somethin' about it here that I'm not gonna be able to forget." "The last ten days have been awesome but I told Douglas last night when we were at the hospital, I already know that there's gonna be some issues because of where I am now."

"He's not gonna have a problem with it is he?"

"He might because just like you were talkin' the other day about how it was right after Douglas got the Holy Ghost, it's gonna be the same way but I'm sorry, I can't go back."

"And when he sees that you might be surprised at what it does for him, just don't try to force anything on him because that won't work." She said as Douglas came up from outside.

"It really doesn't, I heard that." He said as he sat down.

"You have to be right because nobody would ever be able to tell that you almost broke up."

"I came this close." Irene said as she put her thumb and index fingers together. "Then Paul got hold of me and got in my face and made me think twice about that because I was totally fed up."

"About what if you don't mind me askin.'" "I'm just tryin' to understand because how could you be upset about somethin' that's so wonderful Irene?" She asked, shaking her head. "I'm not gettin' it." She said, laughing with them.

"Because me and my hardheaded self was in love with the world and I knew that he wasn't gonna be goin' to the clubs and runnin' the streets and whatever else we were doin' and my feelin's were seriously hurt."

"And I think she really got the message that I wasn't playin' when I wouldn't use my offerin' money to get groceries in the house one time."

"I was hot and I think that day was the first time in my life that I let out a few cuss words because I just couldn't understand how in the world he could do that." "And I learned that potty mouth stuff from him, I didn't know how to say bad words 'til I met him."

"But then two days later, somebody put a fifty dollar bill in my hand." Douglas said, still laughing with them. "I put twenty dollars in the offferin' that day and got fifty back, do the math." "The Lord is not gonna be outdone, I don't care how it looks." He said as he passed Marie a napkin as she cried and laughed at the same time.

"Do you see what I mean now, it was that kind of stuff that was blowin' my mind." Irene said. "I mean I couldn't find junkyard nowhere and I wasn't used to livin' like that, even though I saw mother go through some of the same kind of things when we were growin' up."

"Then what was it that finally made you give it up?" Marie asked as she wiped her eyes.

"I finally got a revelation one day after I got through cussin' and cryin' and carryin' on about somethin' I didn't like that he did, I don't even remember what it was now." She began. "But after I got through throwin' my little tantrum, he came up to me and said but I still love you and that's when I lost it." "I was done after that because I still remembered how it was before and this was totally opposite from what I was used to."

"That is so awesome Irene, I'm gonna remember that for a long time."

"But I should've known all along that this is real, mother wouldn't let us skip church for nothin' so I knew what was up."

"You don't really know what's up 'til it happens to you." Douglas said. "You can be around it all of your life like she was but 'til you actually make that connection with the power of God, you just don't know."

"And I tried to tell Jerry about it but I couldn't really explain to him what happened to me on April first."

"I got a chance to talk to him that Sunday night and I don't know how much he might remember but we'll be prayin' for you and your mother, you'll be okay."

"Am I gonna get to meet your brother before we leave, is he here?"

"He's out lookin' for a job, he's been on line sendin' out applications and he'll probably be back before you leave tonight." Irene told her.

"Did Janice come with you?" Douglas asked her.

"She's down in the basement kitchen gettin' stuff together." Irene said. "Did you get the ice?" She asked Douglas.

"It's already down there, I got this."

"How many kids are you expectin' to be here?" Marie asked.

"Fifteen or twenty maybe so it'll be loud down there." Irene said. "Brace yourself."

"Are you gonna let me show you my bedroom over there?" Michael asked Janice after sneaking up behind her in the kitchen as she worked at the corner countertop. "And how's that baby in there?" He asked her after kissing the back of her neck.

"You need to stop it, I am not doin' that." She said after quickly turning around.

"You did it once so you'll do it again." He said angrily as he walked out. "Let me know when you're ready."

"I almost told Douglas what happened but then I thought that it might start somethin' between them so that's why I'm tellin' you." Janice said as she sat at the table with Chris and James around midnight. "I had to tell somebody."

"Do you want me to tell him?" James asked her as he twirled a salt shaker around. "If you do, I won't have a bit of a problem talkin' to him."

"He might already know." Chris said, half kidding.

"Probably not but here's the thing." James said. "This happened in his house and he might not say a word to him about it but he has the right to know what went on."

"He was ready, if I had said okay, he wouldn't have had any problem with it at all." Janice said, thinking back to the moment. "Then when I told him that he needed to stop it, he got really mad and told me to let him know when I was ready because if I did it once, he said that I would do it again." She said as she wiped a small tear out of the corner of one of her eyes.

"And you told him that you don't do that anymore." Chris said.

"I just said that I wasn't doin' it." She recalled. "It was like he couldn't believe it."

"Like somebody was actually standin' up to him."

She nodded. "And I know that type of guy, Craig was like that and that's probably why I'm sittin' here pregnant now and I'm so glad that I didn't have any problem tellin' him to back off of me." "I know this works now because I felt God in there with me."

"Did you have any doubt about it before?" James asked her.

"No I didn't because I know what I felt when I first got the Holy Ghost but now I know for myself that it's a lot deeper than that."

"You passed one of your first tests and when Douglas finds this out, he's gonna be so proud of you." Chris told her.

"And when he told me yesterday when we were talkin' at the hospital that he was probably gonna do somethin' like this, I didn't really wanna believe it."

"Hold up, hold up." James said suddenly. "Let me get this straight; he told you that Michael was probably gonna do what he did?"

"He said that the Lord had led him to talk to me about this and to make sure that I knew that we don't have sex unless you're married." She said. "And it's a good thing we talked because I wasn't quite sure about that but he could tell by the way he was checkin' me out the other day what he was thinkin'."

"Because Douglas has been around the block a few times, he was warnin' you." Chris said. "And I noticed it too but you have to be really careful, which is why he hasn't said anything to Michael before now." "He came to you with it and that's nothin' but wisdom and I just love that about him." "You have to think things through before you go flyin'

off the handle about stuff;he was doin' what the world does so how can you judge him when he doesn't know anything about holiness and fornication?" "I'm not defendin' him but that's the way I see it."

"Are you finished ma'am?" James asked her as he took one of her hands."I love you too and I agree with everything you just said baby but Douglas is Janice's father now and he needs to know what happened in his house and I wouldn't feel right not tellin' him." "And the best way to avoid any more trouble like this is to make sure that you stay away from him and not give him the chance to try that again." He told Janice. "It's simple and if you don't have a problem with it, I'll talk to him if you don't feel comfortable with it." "Some things are just better man to man, you know what I mean?"

She nodded.

"Don't you think you'll feel better when he knows?" Chris asked her. "He probably won't be surprised since he warned you about him and he did that because he's lookin' out for you." "And don't worry about them gettin' into it because he hasn't forgotten where he came from and he knows how to talk to people, especially his brother."

"I don't know what I would do without you guys." Janice said then.

"That's why you're here and we're glad that you decided to stay so don't ever feel like you're in the way." Chris told her. "And I know what I forgot to tell you."

"What?" She asked cautiously.

"Have you called the maternal and infant clinic at the hospital yet?" "You need to get your prenatal care started because October isn't that far off."

She nodded. "And I think I felt it move the other day so I guess it's time."

"Your health insurance should kick in pretty soon too so it's all good; no worries."...

CHAPTER 11

MONDAY, APRIL 13

"They got back home around ten-thirty and Marie is sendin' a life insurance check that she got in the mail while she was here." Janice remarked after she and Douglas sat down in the main sanctuary after he dismissed a youth meeting Monday evening.

"Be sure to call your mother once a week so she won't think that you've forgotten about her." He said. "And let's cut to the chase ma'am, did James tell you that he talked to me yesterday about Michael?"

"He did and I guess I feel better that you know about it but I don't wanna make a bigger deal out of it than it is, I think he knows now that I'm not goin' there with him."

"That's a good thing and you made the right move by tellin' him that but that's not a guarantee that he won't try it again so don't let your guard down." He told her. "And James had the right idea when he said to keep it simple by just stayin' away from him but I don't want you to feel like that we're tryin' to control you either."

"I don't, but I don't want him to feel like we think we're better than him and all of that either." She said. "I was thinkin' about what Chris said when I told her and James and she was right."

"He told me what she said and that's exactly why I'm not sayin' a word to him about it, I think you got that job done but if it happens again, there would have to be some changes made." He said as his phone vibrated. "So stay encouraged and keep doin' what you're doin'." He said as she stood up to leave. "You did good." He said as she gave him a quick hug.

"Hey man, it's me." Michael said after he answered.

"What's goin' on?" He asked him as he started walking out of the sanctuary.

"Man I'm downtown, I just got pulled over for speedin' and they took my car because I didn't pass the breathalyzer thing." He said with a slight slur. "You need to come and get me man."

"They're not holdin' you, just the car?"

"Man they can't hold me, I don't have a record." He said, raising his voice.

"Give me an hour Michael, I need to get James so we can get your car out of hock."

"You know where I am man?"

"I know exactly where you are, give me an hour." He told him again right before he ended the call.

"I know there's a part of you that wants to wring his neck but you just can't do that." James said as he and Douglas sat in his van outside after Michael went in the house around ten o' clock. "Chris got us told the other night."

"Janice told me about that but what this is doin' is showin' me exactly what I was when I was his age and it's not a pretty picture." He began. "When we went down there to get him, it just reminded me of the times that I ended up in the same place for one thing or another so what I need to do is make sure that I'm not on some kind of self righteous high horse that forgot where he came from."

"Yeah he's goin' through and this is his way of handlin' it but you can't just sit back and not let him know that it doesn't have to be like this." James told him.

"He may not remember a lot of this and I can't really talk to him 'til he sobers up but in the meantime, just keep him in your prayers because I have a feelin' that this is just the beginnin.'"

"Are you feelin' better honey?" Irene asked Michael around midnight as he came out of his room and walked towards the kitchen.

"My head is poundin', you have any coffee in here?" He asked her. "And how come you're still up?"

"This baby of mine is cuttin' teeth and I don't want her keepin' Douglas up so she's down here with me." "I'm waitin' on the pain medicine to kick in."

"So am I the scum of the earth now?" He asked her from the kitchen doorway a half minute later.

"Why would you say that?" "I'm not seein' anything now that I haven't seen before; your brother used to do this almost every weekend and I don't think he would mind me tellin' you that because it is what it is."

"You are kiddin' me." He said.

"Fix yourself a cup of coffee and let me talk to you." She told him.

"Are you about to lecture me?" He asked her as he sat down next to her on the sofa five minutes later.

"I lecture the kids but you are far from anybody's child so I don't do that and I almost feel like I'm sittin' here talkin' to Douglas when he was your age." "All you need is a beard and it would be like goin' back in time." She said in an attempt to put him at ease.

"I had no clue that he was ever into stuff like this, all I really know is what David has told me and the biggest thing he would talk about was all of the women he always had." He said, referring to their older brother.

"Yeah that too but I made sure that that wasn't goin' on once we really started to get serious." She said, starting to recall. "But you're probably not gonna hear much from him about this because he knows that he's been there and done that himself and he doesn't have anything to gain by doggin' you out or kickin' you while you're down." "We know that this is not you."

"If it's not me how did I end up in handcuffs in the back of a squad car Irene?"

"Because stuff happens and if this is enough to keep you from doin' it again, then it'll be worth it."

"I can't say that I will or won't because if somethin' doesn't give, I might end up in the same crap again." He began as he started to vent his frustrations to her. "I haven't worked in almost a month, and nothin' much is openin' up and then on top of that when I get kicked to the curb by a drop dead pretty woman, what's left is a few drinks."

"When it rains it pours huh?"

"And you know it so there it is, you do what you have to do to get over." He said. "And I'm sorry if I'm intrudin' into you and Douglas' storybook Hallmark lifestyle but like you said, it is what it is."

"We have problems like everybody else Michael but when you have the help of God, it makes all the difference." She told him. "And I know that probably doesn't mean that much to you right now but that's how we're gettin' over and dealin' with stuff."

"So does that have anything to do with the way Janice acted with me the other day?" He asked. "How is she gonna act like I'm poison when she obviously let some other dude get over on her?"

"Yeah that's pretty much the reason why she won't go there with you, and it doesn't have anything to do with you personally but she got pregnant before she moved here and got the Holy Ghost."

"Yeah I heard somethin' about that when all of those kids were here Saturday." He said. "How long has she been here?"

"Just a couple of months but a lot has happened to her since and it might seem like she's kickin' you to the curb but it's deeper than that." "She's serious about her salvation and part of that means waitin' 'til you're married before you go to bed with somebody and as strange as that probably seems to you, that's a God thing."

"Is that in the bible somewhere or somethin'?" He asked with sarcasm.

"It is but if you don't believe what's in there or if you don't have any respect for it, it won't make any sense to you." Irene said with understanding patience.

"So I just made a fool out of myself because of some church stuff." He said with aggrevation in his voice.

"You just didn't know Michael and she realizes that so don't feel like that."

"Do you think I owe her an apology?" He asked after a moment.

"If you feel like that's what you should do then go for it but I don't think she's expectin' you to."

"I might do that but what is this thing with her and Douglas?" He asked.

"Since she's been here, he's been able to help her out with a lot of things and she pretty much considers him to be like her father." Irene said. "And since he's old enough to actually be her father, it's not like it could be anything else."

"Didn't I hear that her real father just died?"

"About three weeks ago so it's pretty fresh but she's makin' it because she has a lot more strength than she did when she first came." She told him. "And I didn't tell you that my mother asked me about you yesterday."

"That's interesting." He said wearily. "She doesn't know me like that."

"That doesn't make her any difference so when she gets the chance she'll probably talk your ear off."

"What else am I doin', maybe she could knock some sense into my head because right now I'm feelin' like a piece of you know what."

"And when you feel like that, that's when you can get your help and like it or not, we all need it so there's no point in actin' like we're all that because we're not."

"I'm just used to gettin' what I want when I want it and when that's not happenin', I don't like it." "I'm not used to livin' like this and I don't understand what else I need to do to get out of this; I mean every place that I've applied to is wantin' somebody that has all of this experience and you have to take a drug test to get hired and I'm not goin' there."

"That's just about everywhere but if you're not on drugs, that shouldn't be a problem."

He didn't say anything but shrugged a little before he got up and started back to his room. "I'll see you in the mornin.'"

APRIL 15, WEDNESDAY

"Honey you can come to the back door, I thought maybe I was in trouble from somebody." Frances told Michael after she let him in the front door Wednesday afternoon. "You're family, come to the back." She told him again. "Did Irene tell you that I asked about you on Sunday?" She asked as he followed her back into the kitchen.

"Yes ma'am she did so I thought maybe I needed to come and see you." He said as he sat down hard at the breakfast nook.

"You look like you're hungry, have you eaten anything today?" She asked him.

"I had a hot dog last night left over from the meetin' they had over there Saturday night because I don't feel right eatin' the stuff that Irene cooks everyday." "I don't have an appetite anyway so it's okay."

"No it's not okay honey, you can't keep on like this." Frances told him as she sat down across from him. "You'll get sick and that's the last thing you need so if I fix you a plate will you eat it for me?"

"I don't think I have much of a choice do I?"

"I can't make you eat but I don't know why you wouldn't." She said as she got back up and went towards the refrigerator. "Sheila made some lasagna last night and there's plenty of it here so there's no reason why you can't help us eat it."

"So this is the place to come if you want a plate huh?"

"I don't turn anybody down because I have more than enough and I don't want food to go to waste." She said. "How's the job thing goin' for you?"

"It's not and I know that I've applied to twenty places or more since I've been here and I'm tryin' to figure out what the problem is with me." "And I hopin' that what happened Monday night won't make it worse but I don't have anybody to blame for that but myself."

"What happened honey?"

"You mean it's not all over town yet?"

"It must not be 'cause I don't know anything about it." She said as she cut a large slice of lasagna and put it on a plate.

"I was out drivin' around Monday night tryin' to learn my way around here and I got pulled over for speedin' and flunked the breathalyzer test." He spit out. "I called Douglas to come and pick me up from downtown somewhere and he hasn't said a word about it for two days."

"Did you think that he was gonna jump down your throat because of it?" She asked him as she put the plate in the microwave.

"I was bracin' myself because I know what he's about." "But Irene told me the other night that I probably wouldn't hear any more about it from him because he's been in the same place."

"She was absolutely right and the stories that I could tell you would probably shock you but I won't do that because all of that is under the blood of Jesus and it wouldn't accomplish anything." She told him. "Now if he would choose to tell you about some of the things that God saved him from, that's up to him but I love and respect him too much to do that."

"I understand." Michael said after a moment.

"And he loves you enough not to rub stuff in your face because none of us has the right to be judge and jury over anybody." She told him as she set a glass of ice water in front of him. "But I will tell you this, he does have the right to say what goes on in his house but you probably know that by now so I won't mess with that."

"Yeah I found that out the hard way too with Janice and I almost feel like I owe her an apology."

"Did they talk to you about that?" She asked him as she went back over to the microwave to get his plate out.

"Yeah I'm gettin' a real education about stuff around here." He said, shaking his head a little. "I mean I don't exactly understand what the big deal is because when a guy sees a girl that looks like she does, you go after it; that's just what we do, let's keep it real."

"And it's because of that that you're gonna see how protective Douglas is of her because she's so vulnerable."

"I didn't get that feelin' about her but if you say so, I'm gonna trust you, you know her a lot better than I do." He said. "I don't know her at all but that didn't stop me from bein' attracted to her."

"And there is nothin' wrong with that honey and the day might come when it all works out but right now, she's just not in a place where she's available to you."

"Because of the church thing huh?" He asked.

"I don't even think that I would call it that but the very thing that happened the other night is just an example of the problems that would come up." Frances said after a moment. "When one of you has the spirit of God and the other one doesn't, it's like mixin' oil and water, it doesn't work like it's supposed to." "You have two different mindsets tryin' to work together and most of the time, it doesn't work." "When Douglas came home with the Holy Ghost, the stuff hit the fan because it brought about a division between them and she came really close to leavin' him because of it."

"That's pretty deep; I don't get it but because you said it, I'm tryin' to piece it all together." He said shaking his head again. "And don't get me wrong, I really do appreciate you talkin' to me like this because I've been goin' crazy tryin' to figure it all out."

"All of this is a lot to deal with at one time and what we need to do is believe that the Lord will work all of this out because you're not here by accident." She told him. "God has a way of allowing things to happen that seem to be pretty bad on the surface but by the time things fall into place, it's worth every bit of the trouble that you went through."

"How can anything good come out of this?"

"When you have lived through as much as I have you see how faithful God is and it doesn't matter that you're as young as you are; He will do things for you even when He's the last thing on your mind." She told him. "It's called mercy and grace and every last one of us see it when you wake up in the mornin' and didn't die in your sleep."

"If this is all I'm wakin' up to every mornin', I don't know if that's a good thing or not." Micheal said. "And I'm tryin' to listen to everything you're tellin' me but it's hard to wrap my head around anything positive right now." "I'm not used to livin' on the edge and havin' to depend on other people to get by, this kind of stuff happens to other people, not me."

"But it is you honey and you have to be thankful that it's not any worse because it certainly could be." She told him. "How would you like to be layin' up in the morgue somewhere with your soul in

Eternity without salvation?" "It's happenin' everyday so while you have life in you, take advantage of it and let God help you."

He didn't speak but nodded a little in acknowledgement."

"And just so you know, I'm not comin' down on you for the sake of talkin' because I had to say the same things to your brother and he was in a lot worse shape than you are." "He was ready to blow his brains out because he saw one of his best friends die right in front of him on a motorcycle." "The guy lost his head out on the street and it messed his mind up to the point where he wasn't eatin' or sleepin' and Irene called me cryin' her heart out because she felt so helpless." "And baby that's when God stepped in and got a hold of him and he hasn't been the same since."

"Wow, that's deep." "He never told me about that one."

"The next time you talk to him, ask him about it because I can only tell you about it from what I remember." "But he lived through it and he's the only one that can put into words how the Lord got him out of the wilderness he was in but you don't want to get to that point, so now is the time for you to give it up and give it to God because pity parties don't get you anywhere."

"When I told Irene that you could probably knock some sense into me, I didn't think it would be like this but I hear you." He said then as he finished his plate.

"I'm talkin' to you like this because for some reason the Lord has laid you on my heart and it's been like that from the day you first walked in here with Douglas." She told him. "And we're gonna stop right here and have a word of prayer for you and your situations because there's nothin' too big or hard for God to do." She said as she stood up, walked over to the other side of the table and gently placed her hands on his shoulders and began to thank God for hearing and answering her petitions on his behalf. He then began to react to the anointing of the spirit of God that he felt through her touch by openly and unashamedly crying out tears of frustration, guilt, fear and helplessness.

"And I'm callin' it all done in the name of Jesus." She whispered to him as he sat there in stunned silence at what he had just felt for the first time in his life. "Just sit right here for as long as you want to and let God help you." She told him as the phone on the wall rang.

"Aunt Frances it's me." Sheila said after she answered it a moment later.

"What's goin' on honey, where are you?"

"I'm right outside in my car." "Did you know that Uncle William is out here sittin' in his car passed out?"

"Is he in the driveway or the street?" She asked her after digesting what she had just told her. "Are you sure that it's him?"

"Yes ma'am, it's him and he's parked right in front of the mailbox." "Is that Michael's car in the driveway?"

"Yeah he's here, he just had some of your lasagna." She said calmly. "I need to call Paul." She added after thinking a moment.

"School is out around three thirty so you might be able to get him before he goes home." "Or I can call him, I have his number in my phone."

"Call him for me and tell him I said to get here as soon as he can." "Are you sure that he's not just sleepin'?"

"The car door is part of the way open like he tried to get out and just couldn't make it." She told her. "He's sort of slumped over."

"Maybe I need to come out there and see what's goin' on with him." "Stay there, I'm on my way out."

"He can't stay here like this mother, he's sick as a dog." Paul told her an hour later after he and Michael got William into the house and in bed. "Did you call everybody else?"

"Sheila went to get Donna and the kids and Irene and Chris are comin' later when Douglas and James get home."

"How long has it been since he was here the last time?" Paul asked her a few minutes later as they sat down in the kitchen.

"He was here about three years ago and he was gone before I knew it." "He left a five hundred dollar check in the mailbox and that was the last I've heard anything from him 'til today." Frances said as she stirred in a cup of coffee. "He looks like he's lost about fifty pounds and I'm not exaggeratin'."

"Because he's sick and I don't know what it is that he has but we can't let you wear yourself down tryin' to take care of him." "I need to talk to Irene and Chris and Donna and we're gonna have to come up with a plan." "He probably needs to be in the hospital." He said as Donna and Sheila came in the back door.

"Are you okay mother?" Donna asked as she came over to her.

"I'm fine honey, this is not the first time this has happened, but he's never shown up sick like this before."

"I need to see my girl!" William yelled out then from the bedroom.

"This is the first thing he's said since he's been here." Frances said as they both got up and went to the room.

"William, calm down." Frances told him a minute later as Paul attempted to keep him from falling out of the bed.

"You need to let me see my girl before I die! He insisted.

"Donna's here and Chris and Irene are on their way." Paul told him.

"I need to see Kathryn's girl, that's my girl!" He yelled again as he began to sob. "That's my baby!"

"I can't hardly believe that this is happenin.'" Chris remarked an hour later as she, Irene and Donna sat in the living room. "This is the kind of stuff that happens on a soap opera, this is crazy."

"Chris it's crazy but it's true and we just have to deal with it." Irene told her. "Janice is our half sister instead of our cousin, plain and simple."

"Maybe he's just talkin' out of his head." Chris commented.

"No he's not." Irene said. "When you start to put two and two together, it's really simple how this happened."

"I'm listenin.'"

"He's been comin' and goin' like this since you were a baby Donna and you're what, twenty-nine?"

She nodded a little.

"For some strange reason, him and Aunt Kathryn hooked up about this time nineteen years ago when her and uncle Roy were separated for a minute and nine months later, here comes Janice." Irene said. "Cut and dried, there it is. "Irene said, shaking her head.

"Has mother called Aunt Kathryn yet?" Donna asked.

"She's in there talkin' to her now because she wants to be sure that it's really true." Chris said. "And this is probably why Uncle Roy treated her like he did, he knew that she wasn't his."

"It's all comin' together and when she finds this out, it's not gonna be a pretty picture." Irene said as Paul walked in.

"Is mother still on the phone?" Chris asked him.

"Yeah she is and we finally got him to settle down but he's not gonna be satisfied until he sees her and I don't know how that's gonna work." "She might not even feel comfortable with that and I don't think I would blame her."

"But she has to know and it'll be up to her whether she does that or not but this whole thing is so bizarre that it doesn't feel real." Chris said.

"We just need to stop bein' so dramatic about it and get it done." Irene said. "She's stronger than we think she is." She added as Frances came in with an expression of calm resignation on her face.

"You have another sister, she's not your cousin, she's your half sister." She told them as she sat down next to Chris.

"Are you okay mother?" Donna asked her as she wiped her face.

"Honey, I'm fine and after talkin' to Kathryn, you might have some more brothers and sisters all over the country that you'll never know about but this one you do and she needs to find out."

"Was she surprised that you know about it now?"

"When she answered the phone, she thought maybe somethin' was goin' on with Janice because I'm not in the habit of callin' her in the middle of the day like this." She began. "Then I told her that William just showed up here and said that he needed to see his girl before he dies and that's when she goes dead silent."

"And that's when you knew that he wasn't just talkin' out of his head." Chris said.

"That's when I knew, she didn't have to say another word but that just told me that you have another sister." "Her and Roy were separated for about six months and by the time they got back together, she was probably four or five months pregnant with Janice which lets us know why he treated her so different than he did Marie." "He knew she wasn't his so why should he act like it, that was his thinkin.'"

"That's exactly what I just said but why would he even go back to her knowin' that she was carryin' somebody else's baby?" Irene said. "I don't get that, I'm sorry."

"Maybe they got back together because of Marie, I didn't ask her that but there it is."

"I need to see my girl!" William yelled out again.

"Somebody needs to get her here because he might do this all night long." Paul said as he started back towards the room.

"I'll have James bring her over here, 'Nita can stay with the kids for a minute." Chris said then. "I'll call her first and tell her that we need to talk to her about somethin.'"

"Am I in trouble or somethin'?" Janice asked half an hour later after she and James came in the back door.

"No honey you're not in trouble, we just found out some news that you need to know about." Frances told her.

"Where's everybody else?" James asked as he came over to hug her.

"They're in there with William, they figured that I needed to be by myself." She said, folding up the newspaper. "Are you feelin' okay?" She asked Janice as she sat down.

"Yes ma'am." "When did he come home?"

"This afternoon and we found out today that he's your father honey, Roy wasn't." Frances told her. Irene, Chris and Donna are your half sisters, not your cousins." "And Paul is your half brother."

"Can you say that again, I don't think I'm understandin.'" Janice said after a moment, obviously confused.

"Do you remember when I told you how the kids father would come and go whenever he felt like it for the last thirty years?" Frances asked her.

She nodded a little after thinking a moment.

"Well it was probably about this time nineteen years ago that him and your mother got together and made you honey." "I called her to make sure that it was true because all he's been talkin' about is seein' you because he's really sick and he may not be around too much longer."

"You mean they had some kind of fling and that's how I got here?" She said as she felt herself start to react in a negative way but allowed the power of her spirit to constrain her from any unseemly behaviour.

"In a nutshell that's pretty much it but we don't want you to feel like you're obligated to go in there to see him." "If you think that it would make you too uncomfortable, just say so and that would be the end of it."

"How does this make you feel Janice?" Paul asked her then as he came in the kitchen.

She didn't answer as she sat there and started to let her mind go back to the years of emotional abuse and neglect that she had endured from Roy coupled with the deceit that Kathryn had allowed to go on for her entire life.

"Do you need to talk to your sisters in there?" Frances asked her. "They're still tryin' to process this just like you are and they're more worried about you than anything else." She said. "And don't worry about how I'm dealin' with it because I haven't really had a husband for years so I'm not really feelin' this like you are."

"Why didn't she just tell me this a long time ago?" She asked helplessly. "If I had known this, then I wouldn't have wondered why he acted so different with Marie when we were kids." She barely got out as she looked up and noticed Douglas walk in and come towards them.

"Sweetheart this is your father that the Lord has given you so don't let all of that mess you up." Frances told her as she scooted over to make room for him. "We know that all of that hurts but this isn't somethin' that can be undone so all we can do is move on from this."

She nodded a little as she began to call on the ever present help in time of trouble before she allowed herself to "get it all out of her system" by completely letting herself go as years of pent up anxiety came to the surface.

It was then that Douglas got back up, went to her side and helped her to stand up as he instinctively understood the effects of being deprived of a true father all of her eighteen years. As he allowed her to "lean on him", he gently escorted her into the livingroom where she sat down while he went to get Irene and Chris from the bedroom where William continued to be combative and insistent on seeing her.

"Janice are you okay honey?" Irene asked her a minute later as they came and sat down on either side of her.

"I will be, it just all came out at one time but I'm okay." She said. "And I feel sort of bad that Douglas came all the way over here but it really did help." She added.

"When I called and told him what was goin' on, he got hold of Sheila and she's with the kids so don't worry about it." Irene told her.

"And if you don't feel like goin' in there to see him, that's okay too." Chris said. "How do you feel about that?"

"Does it have to be now?" She asked them. "Tomorrow might be better, I need time to think about this."

"We need to get him in the hospital, he just had a bad accident in there, he can't be here." Donna said, coming in then.

"There's your answer honey, tomorrow might be better"...

CHAPTER 12

APRIL 16, THURSDAY

"We ran several tests on him and at this point, he'll be going up to hospice care from here." William's doctor spoke to Paul and Frances Thursday afternoon. "We found that he has stage four colon cancer and there may be some kidney failure also that's complicating everything else so there's really nothing that we can do except keep him comfortable."

"Nobody knows when they're leavin' here but how long do you think he might have?" Frances asked him then.

"We're probably looking at a week or two, not any longer than that to be really honest with you." He concluded. "So if I were you, I would get any family members together that want to see him because he's actually drifting in and out of consciousness, and he may not realize that anyone is even in the room with him."

Paul nodded then as they stood up to go back towards the I.C.U. area.

"So if you have any questions or concerns, we have a hospice staff here that is available twenty four hours a day."

"Have you talked to Janice since last night?" Paul asked her as they walked down the hallway a few minutes later.

"She called me early this mornin' and her and Irene are comin' out here this evenin' to see him, she said that she thought about it and it might help her get over this whole thing."

"Has she talked to Kathryn yet?"

"Probably not and it might be a while before she's ready to do that and at this point, I'm ready to move on, nothin' can change this so it is what it is."

"I was sittin' there after Aunt Frances told me what was goin' on, and I guess I was in some kind of shock or somethin' and then just all of a sudden, he just showed up out of nowhere." Janice remarked in the kitchen with Irene after James dropped her off after work.

"How did that make you feel?" Irene asked as she sat down to feed Annette in her high chair.

"It was a little scary because it was just so right on time and then when she said that this is my father that the Lord gave me, that's when I really lost it." She said as she recalled her words. "I felt like I was five years old and I just hope he doesn't think I was crazy actin' but that's the way it was and I already knew it but it was somethin' about the way she said it kind of made it official." "I was feelin' like I was just out there."

"He didn't think that because he told me later on that he was glad that you felt free enough to be yourself and there's nothin' wrong with that." "And don't ever feel that you're imposin' or gettin'in the way because you need somebody that you can trust and respect." "And we didn't get that because he was gone so much of the time."

"So how was Aunt Frances makin' it without him around?"

"She used to tell us all of the time that the Lord was her husband and we thought that sounded off or crazy but I can sort of see what she meant now." Irene said after a moment. "We always had what we needed and we learned how to be independent because we didn't really have a choice."

"But all four of you are doin' really good so it must be a God thing." Janice said. "I hear Sheila sayin' that all of the time and it's rubbin' off on me."

"But a lot of things just are, we can't take the credit for some of the stuff that we see happen so they're God things." Irene said as Michael walked in, unaware that Janice was there.

"I'm sorry, I didn't know you had company Irene." He said as he turned around and started back out.

"You don't have to leave Michael, c'mon back in here." Irene told him. "We don't bite."

"How's it goin'?" Janice asked him as she noticed his obvious discomfort at the awkward moment.

"Not bad actually." He said, as he cautiously sat down at the table. "I finally have an interview set up for tomorrow and I can't believe how quick they called me back."

"Mother told me that you stopped by there yesterday." Irene said.

"She let me have it and made me think about some stuff." He began. "Then when she got through talkin', she got to prayin' for me and I started to feel stuff that I have never felt before and I thought I had been around the block a few times." He said, shaking his head, while still avoiding eye contact with Janice. "She had me cryin' like a baby and I don't ever do that."

"Sometimes it happens like that so you think maybe she got a prayer through for you?" Irene asked him.

"If this job opens up for me, then I'm gonna start thinkin' that somebody's tryin' to tell me somethin.'" He said. "And I've heard people say that God answers prayer but I never have thought that much about it 'til now."

"They broke ground on Paul and Jane's house the other day so James might be callin' you too pretty soon so stop stressin' out." Irene told him.

"Have you heard anything else about your father?"

"Paul called this mornin' and they're puttin' him in hospice care; he's probably got a couple of weeks." She said after a moment. "We're goin' to the hospital when Douglas gets here."

"So you found out that you're actually half sisters huh?' He asked Janice in an attempt to break the tension that he felt.

She nodded. "And we decided not to call it half because it would be like a reminder of this whole thing."

"I've got to get ready to go Janice, we're leavin' as soon as Douglas gets here." Irene said as she picked Annette up out of the high chair and started out.

"I think she did that on purpose." Michael said. "I told her the other day that I need to apologize for the other night down there."

"That's over with and we know that it's not gonna happen again so it's all good." She told him. "We'll just act like it never happened."

"Just like that huh?"

She nodded. "If I had to apologize to somebody for somethin' that I did, I wouldn't want to hear about it again so it works both ways."

"Are you sure that you're just eighteen?" He asked her after listening to the maturity of her answer and attitude.

"I turned eighteen in February but when you've been through some stuff, you have to grow up." She said. "But last night, like I told Irene a few minutes ago, I felt like I was five years old again when Douglas just showed up out of nowhere right when I was seriously trippin' about this." "And he didn't say anything at all but it was the way he knew exactly what to do and I know that that had to be the Lord, it just had to be." She said with emphasis.

"That's really some deep stuff right there."

"It is because I was startin' to feel like I was out there by myself and then after that happened, all of that went somewhere else and I'm not lettin' it come back either."

"I think you mean that."

"I do mean that because if I let myself go back to what I was when I first moved here I would be crazy." She said. "I didn't trust anybody and the only reason I came here was because I couldn't think of anywhere else to go and that was God too." "If James and Chris hadn't let me stay there with them, I might've ended up in a shelter somewhere, I would've probably got an abortion and I wouldn't have the Holy Ghost either, I know that for sure."

"So did they talk you out of it or somethin'?"

"They didn't even know it 'til I was here probably a month and I was sittin' here complainin' to Douglas because I couldn't find a job." "I was here to babysit the next day because Irene had to be somewhere and he could tell that I was sittin' on somethin' else but I was scared to tell anybody because I was afraid that I would get the same thing that I did from my mother when I told them." "So I was around here stressin' out, tryin' to figure out how I was gonna let somebody know before I started to show."

"Did he guess?"

She shook her head. "I just let it out when he asked me if somethin'else was botherin' me and I sat right here in this same seat and cried like I was two years old." She said, thinking back to the moment. "And then I look up and see him wipin' tears off of his face and that tripped me out even more."

"You are kiddin' me." Michael said in mild shock. "I don't feel so bad now." He said, laughing a little as he listened to her with fascination.

She nodded. "And then when I said it wasn't too late to do somethin' about it, he told me that that wasn't an option and he was so serious that it was a little scary." "But I knew then that this was somebody that actually cared about what I was goin' through and I wasn't used to that."

"So is that when you told Chris and James?"

"He got on the phone and called Chris and told her because I was too scared to tell 'em myself and that's when I found out how real they are too." Janice said. "They have been my angels and now that I know that she's my sister instead of my cousin like we thought, it makes it a lot easier for me to talk to her or whatever I need to do." She finished as Douglas came in.

"Well this is different." He said as he set his laptop on the counter. "Is everything okay?"

"Yeah man, she's safe; I'm just gettin' a better understandin' of some stuff." He said as he stood up to leave, sensing that he needed to talk with her.

"He thinks I'm the boogey man and that might not be such a bad thing." Douglas said as he sat down. "And I know that you and Irene are goin' out to the hospital but if you don't feel comfortable tryin' to talk to him, don't put any pressure on yourself." He told her.

She nodded a little. "I've been tryin' to think about what I can say but I don't know him so that makes it kind of hard, you know what I mean?" She said after a moment. "And Aunt Frances said they told her and Paul that he might not even know that we're there."

"He might not but you can't really count on that." He told her. "But you're strong enough to deal with whatever he might say so don't be too surprised at what you might hear."

"Chris told me the same thing so I'm sort of bracin' myself."

"Have you thought about callin' your mother yet?"

"I'm tryin' to give it a little more time because I can see myself gettin' upset again but I'm prayin' about that too because I feel like I'd be goin' backwards instead of lettin' it go."

"You're doin' the right thing by allowin' your Holy Ghost to help you because if you let yourself get bitter over this, you're hurtin' yourself plus she wouldn't be able to see the change in you." He told her. "If she sees that you're judgin' her and puttin' her on a guilt trip, then that makes your witness a whole lot less effective."

"I didn't even think about it like that." She admitted.

"Yes ma'am so the best thing for you to do is to let her know that you still love her and that you won't be holdin' anything against her but make sure that you mean it and you're not just sayin' it because it sounds good."

"Wow." She said after thinking for a moment.

"You have what it takes to make a lot of difference in her life and yours too so don't let your adversary the devil eat you alive with this." "When the Lord gave you the Holy Ghost, he set you free and you have enough on your plate without havin' to deal with anything extra." He said as Irene came in.

"Yes you do so we just have to deal with one thing at a time." She said. "And God is in control of all of this so just relax."

"So when did Michael Johnson show up?"

"He didn't know that she was gonna be here and when he came in and saw her, he turned around and was gonna walk right back out but I told him that he didn't have to do that." Irene said as he handed her the car keys.

"He apologized for the other night so he knows what's up." Janice said as she stood up.

"I was just checkin' but if you ever need me to take him to the woodshed, don't hesitate to let me know."

"Can you hear me daddy?" Irene asked William an hour later in his room as Janice sat in a nearby chair.

"Who is that?" He asked after a moment as he opened his eyes. "Irene?" He asked her after looking up at her.

"How do you feel?" She asked him.

"How come I'm in here and where is that other girl I told you I needed to see?" He asked with irritation in his voice.

"She's right here, we didn't forget." She told him as Janice got up and slowly approached his bed.

"Are you my other girl?" He asked her as he he held his hand out to her.

She nodded. "Yes sir." She said as she reluctantly took his hand that felt cold and clammy to her.

"You're such a pretty girl, why didn't Kathryn let me see you sweetheart?" He asked as he began to openly sob. "I'm gonna die in here and she didn't let me see you." He bemoaned.

"But I'm here now." Janice said after a moment as she struggled to think of the appropriate words to say to him.

"I just wanted you to know that I'm your father just like I'm theirs but your mother didn't want me near you girl." He said as he began to cough. "When you was born, I wanted to get a look at you but she wanted to act like she didn't want anything to do with me."

She nodded as she continued to listen to him.

"We got together when her and Roy split up so I didn't break up nobody's house, but she wanted me and I wanted her and that's why you're here but that don't mean that I don't love you the same as the rest of 'em." He said apologetically.

"I understand." She managed to say as she remembered how Douglas had warned her about his choice of words.

"Roy told me to stay away from you too because I messed up things enough and that you didn't need to know that I was your daddy." He continued as he forcefully purged himself of long buried issues of the situation. "She told me that she would tell Frances what happened if I didn't stop tryin' to see you so that's why you don't know me!" He said as he raised his voice.

It was then that Irene noticed how stressful his words were becoming to Janice and as she came over to calm him down and steer her away from him, he became more combative and determined to keep talking to her.

"You really don't need to say anymore, we're done with this." She told him as a nurse walked in after overhearing him.

"Is everything okay in here?" She asked as she went over to his i.v. drip. "William do you need to go to sleep for a while hon?" She asked him as he lay there in regretful repentant tears.

"Do you have a sedative or somethin' that you can give him?" Irene asked her as she noticed Janice walk out.

"I can give him a mild dose just to calm him down so if you need to step out for a few minutes and come back, that's fine."

"You okay?" Irene asked Janice as she found her standing against the wall outside the room.

She nodded, determined not to crumble after what she had just heard from William.

"C'mon, we need to sit down somewhere." She told her, putting an arm around her as they started down the hallway.

"I don't ever need to see or talk to him anymore, that was enough Irene." She said a minute later as they sat down in a waiting area. "I'm done."

"There's really not a lot that you can say, he saw you and you saw him so what else is left?"

"If I had stayed in there and let him keep tellin' me stuff that I don't really need to hear, it would've been bad and I'm just not gonna let myself trip out like that anymore." Janice said with determination.

"Are you gonna tell your mother that you know now?" Irene asked her after a moment.

"I might but not right now, it's too soon." "And Douglas told me that I can't let this make me bitter but I would still sort of like to know why she didn't want him to see me."

"We might not ever know but he's right about that, don't let what she did affect you, that would just bring you down and you don't need that."

"I didn't tell you that I got an insurance check in the mail from Marie the other day and I don't feel right keepin' it so I'll just send it back to her."

"I don't think she knows, have you called her?"

She shook her head a little. "I probably need to because I don't think mother's gonna tell her." She said after thinking a moment.

"If we're finished out here, I need to get you home, you look tired." Irene told her then.

"I am so I need to go home and find somewhere to pray and go to sleep because I'm done.".

April 18, Saturday

"He said that he would call you tonight when they get done out at the lot, he's a little bit in shock." Douglas remarked Saturday morning as he and Frances sat in the kitchen.

"He knows now what prayer can do and he might've gotten the job anyway but I'm sayin' that this is the Lord, no question about it." She said.

"Did he tell you why he ended up over here in the first place?"

"I think Irene told him that I had asked her about him on Sunday and that was because he had just been on my mind for some reason, so he thought he'd come by here." She said as she poured more coffee in his cup.

"So he got his first taste of what it feels like to have the Lord touch you huh?"

"I don't think he'll ever forget it but sometimes that's what it takes to make you come to yourself and you know as well as I do that it's the goodness of God that leads to repentance and that's what he's experiencing, whether he knows it or not."

"Whatever it was that you said to him made a difference and he probably took it better from you than he would've from me so God knows."

"And you know that's right because you're his brother and sometimes it's better comin' from a stranger than from somebody that you're close to." She said. "And I was practically a stranger to him when he first walked in here but he can't say that anymore; I can see me and that young man becomin' best friends."

"That's not a hard thing to do, believe it or not."

"It's just a little hard for me to keep the things that the Lord has taught me under wraps because people are goin' through a lot of crazy things and you need all of the wisdom and knowledge you can get." She said. "And that's one of the reasons that I'm so glad that you and James have stepped up like you have to keep Janice from fallin' apart."

"We know where her help is really comin' from so I don't like to go there like that."

"Of course we know that the Lord is doin' what He does best for her but she has a blessing in you because you're an example of what a father and a strong man should be, regardless of where you used to be Douglas." She told him. "And I don't know whether you noticed it the other day or not, but when she saw you walk in here after what I had just told her, it was like the child in her was sayin' there's my father, everything's gonna be alright now."

"I noticed it which was why I felt like it wasn't necessary to say anything; she already knew and when they went to the hospital the other night, Irene said that William just rubbed salt in the wound by tellin' her stuff that she probably didn't need to hear."

"But she said that you warned her before she went that he might do exactly that so that's why I'm so thankful the Lord gave her the Holy Ghost when He did because He knew this was comin.'"

"So how are you dealin' with all of this?"

"Honey I'm at the place now where I'm pretty numb about it." She said after a moment. "He was gone more than he was here and I would've had to be awfully naïve if I thought that none of that was goin' on." "And like I told the kids, they may have a lot of other half brothers and sisters scattered all over the place that they don't know about but life goes on son."

"You're right about that but we don't want you to be concerned about everybody else and then forget about yourself". He told her. "That's kind of a dangerous thing."

"It is but I know when to pull back and let the Lord help me so don't worry about me." She said. "But I do get concerned that you do the same thing because when people find out that you're the type of person that's willin' to bend over backwards for them, they'll wear you out if you let 'em."

"And like you just said, I know how to pull back and disappear into the woodwork unless the Lord tells me otherwise." He said. "And sometimes it's like that, believe me when I tell you."

"Chris told me about the night that Marie hurt herself and how you just couldn't leave."

"James can tell you about how hard it was for me to get away from there that night." He began. "And when it's like that, I know better than to fight it because God sees the big picture."

"And if you had left, there's no tellin' how that whole thing would've turned out." She said as the phone rang.

"Mother did the hospital call you?" Chris asked her after she answered.

"Is this it?" She asked her after a moment.

"Yeah they called Paul and he died right around ten-thirty they said." "He was just about to go out there when they called him so there it is." "Is anybody with you?"

"Douglas is here with the kids, Irene went to Jane's to help with her garage sale so whenever everybody can get here, let's just do this and see if we can move on."

"I told James to keep workin' out there at the lot and I'm leavin' the kids with Janice and 'Nita.'"

"Does Janice know?"

"Yeah she does but she doesn't think it would do her any good to be there, she'd rather stay here with 'Nita so I'll be there in a few."

"I'm still tryin' to figure it all out because there's too much goin' on too fast for me to understand any of it." Michael remarked as he and James sat in his van at the lot as they took a break. "I've been here less than two weeks and it feels like St. Louis is in another world somewhere."

"Is that a bad or a good thing?"

"It's a crazy thing is what it is because I've never been around so many people that have affected me like this." "I'm used to doin' my own thing and it didn't make any difference what anybody else thought about it but this is another thing altogether." He said, shaking his head. "If you had told me that I would be apologizin' to a girl like I had to do with Janice, I would've told you that you were out of your mind."

"How did that go?" James asked.

"Better than I thought it would and what made it a little easier was the way she made sure I knew she would act like it never happened." He said after thinking a moment. "And that blew my mind because most women that I have had any kind of relationship with would either throw stuff back in your face or hold it over you for somethin' that they wanted out of me."

"How crazy is that?" James said. "I guess I must be out of touch when it comes to stuff like that because Chris is all I've had for the last fifty eleven years as the kids say."

"Man you don't know how lucky you are because it's off the hook crazy out there and when I see how things are around here, it's a little unbelievable, you know what I mean?"

"I can see how it would seem that way if that's all that you're used to but it can be done when you do it the way God intended it to be." James said as he handed him a can of pop from a cooler. "And this that's goin' on out here, I really don't think that it would've happened if I was expectin' Chris to be out there workin' like I am." "And I'm not judgin'anybody that runs their household that way but this was a gift from the Lord, I can't explain it any other way."

"How did this go down, I think Jane tried to explain it to me when I was out here with her a couple of weeks ago but my mind was somewhere else." He admitted.

"Her father was a C.E.O. for a pharmaceutical company and when he died a couple of years ago, everything he had in stocks and bonds and all of that of course went to her mother." He began. "And her thinkin' was that Jane will get everything when she dies anyway so she decided to go out one day to find them a lot to build a bigger house on and here it is."

"And Paul decided to split it with you because this much land was more than what he wanted to take care of."

"There it is, everybody wins." "But then on top of that, she got tired of waitin' on somebody to buy the house that they're in now, so she called their realtor, took him a cashiers check and she's plannin' on usin' it for rental property."

"It sounds like she has more money than she knows what to do with."

"Exactly and her father would have a fit if he knew how her mother was helpin' them out like this because he was a racist." "He didn't come to their wedding or any of that but the Lord has the last say; He moved on that woman's heart and you're lookin' at the results right here and as Douglas tells me all of the time, God is not gonna be outdone, by anybody."

"Irene told me about the time he put twenty dollars in the offerin' one time and she got mad because they didn't have any food in the house." He said laughing. "Then a couple of days later, somebody puts a fifty dollar bill in his hand, just out of nowhere."

"And it's things like that that increase your faith and help you to be obedient when some things just don't seem to make any sense."

"Yeah like the other day when I was at your mother-in-law's house-

"You can call her Aunt Frances like the rest of 'em do." James told him. "Believe me, she would want you to."

He nodded a little as he began to think back to the moment when Frances began to intercede for him and became overwhelmed at the recollection of how her touch had affected him.

"Man it was real, I felt some kind of electricity or somethin' and I know that sounds crazy but I haven't been able to stop thinkin' about it." He said after he gained enough composure to talk again.

"We know what you're talkin' about and there's nothin' else like the power of God and what you felt was just a touch, but if and when you would ever get the Holy Ghost, it would be somethin' that you can't describe."

"That's what Douglas told me one day when we were sort of talkin' about church and all of that and it didn't really make much sense to me but after what I felt the other day, it's a whole new thing." "It was real man." He repeated.

"Tell me about it, I still remember what it felt like when I first realized what was happenin' and you just can't put words to it that are enough to describe it." He said again.

"And then when I get this phone call tellin' me to come in for an interview for this job that starts out payin' twenty dollars an hour, I'm seriously trippin' James." He said, shaking his head again. "And when she was prayin' for me, I can remember her sayin' somethin' about God providin' a job and then two days later, it happens." He finished. "I can't figure it out."

"It's not hard to figure out when you know that the Lord hears and answers prayer and because she had enough faith to intercede for you like she did, He honored that and stepped in and allowed it to happen for you." James told him. "And it might've happened anyway but the result is the same, God is in control."

"And I really do need to get over there again to thank her for doin' that and takin' the time to talk to me like she did because she said some stuff that made me think man."

"She's good at that."

"She started tellin' me that I needed to be glad that I wasn't in the morgue and how Douglas saw his friend die right in front of him and morbid stuff like that." He said, thinking back. "She said he was ready to blow his brains out with a forty-five because he couldn't get that out of his mind and that's some deep stuff."

"And he probably couldn't because she knew how powerful prayer is and he talks about that to people whenever he has the chance because it could've been so different." James said. "The chances are good that you would've lost your brother but God had other plans for him."

"Man like I said, this is some deep stuff and I'm tryin' to wrap my head around all of it so pray for me, I need it.".

APRIL 19, SUNDAY

"I see you're learnin', you came to the back door honey." Frances said as she let Michael in the next morning around ten o' clock.

"I didn't wake you up did I?" He asked as she hugged him.

"I've been up since six, I'm a mornin' person." "Have you had breakfast?"

"I usually don't eat much breakfast but I'll take a cup of coffee if you have some made." "And I meant to call you last night but I knew everybody else was here so I decided to wait 'til now." He said as he sat down. "Are you doin' okay?"

"I actually feel pretty free and we decided that there's not gonna be a funeral so we'll just do a graveside thing Tuesday mornin' at the cemetery and keep it movin' as the kids say." She said as she opened the refrigerator. "And I heard about your good news, didn't I tell you that it was gonna be done?"

"Yes ma'am you did and I was talkin' to James yesterday and I told him that I can't stop thinkin' about what I felt after you got done with me."

"That's because you want more of the same thing and your soul is not gonna leave you alone 'til it's satisfied." She told him. "The Lord allowed you to experience that to let you know that there's a lot more where that came from and it's yours for the asking."

"How is it that you have all of the answers?"

"I don't but I do know a few things about the Lord and He never changes and He keeps His promises." She said as she sat down across from him. "Have you been to church since you've been here?"

"Not yet."

"Well since you're here, why don't I ride with you and I won't have to wait on Paul to pick me up." She said as she got back up. "And the Lord is gonna meet us there."

"This is bigger than I thought it would be." Michael remarked as they started towards the sanctuary entrance half an hour later. "What time do you start?"

"Right around eleven, but we're not watchin' the clock." "Do you need to be somewhere else?"

He shook his head as he once again started to feel the reality of the presence of God the closer they got to the open doors of the auditorium, where unrehearsed singing and praises were going up from thankful, spirit filled people. Then two steps into the sanctuary, he fell prostrate on his face under the power of the Holy Ghost as he totally submitted himself, hungry for the promised Spirit.

As Frances and those close by began to hear the spirit speak through him in a language not his own, she asked an usher to bring Douglas to the back where they were standing around him, rejoicing for one more soul's birthday. A minute later when he realized who it was that they were standing around, it was an undescribable moment to witness as he thought about the seemingly countless intercessory prayers that he had sent up on his behalf. There were no adequate words to speak as they watched him get up on his knees and lift his hands in humble submission to the God of his salvation, who was fluently speaking out of his mouth in an unknown tongue as evidence of His presence in his being.

Half an hour later after his water baptism in the name of Jesus, the church family broke into the anointed song "At the Cross", which invited the presence of the Lord to linger in their midst.

"For the promise is unto you, and to your children, and to all that are afar off, even as many as the Lord our God shall call." (Acts 2:39) KJV.

End of Part 1